STEWARDS OF POWER

RESTORING AFRICA'S DIGNITY

STEWARDS OF POWER

RESTORING AFRICA'S DIGNITY

Dwight S. M. Mutonono

Copyright © 2018 by Dwight S. M. Mutonono

Published 2018 by HippoBooks, an imprint of ACTS and Langham Creative Projects.

Africa Christian Textbooks (ACTS), TCNN, PMB 2020, Bukuru 930008, Plateau State, Nigeria. www.africachristiantextbooks.com

Langham Creative Projects, PO Box 296, Carlisle, Cumbria, CA3 9WZ, UK. www.langham.org

ISBNs:
978-1-78368-405-2 Print
978-1-78368-406-9 ePub
978-1-78368-407-6 Mobi
978-1-78368-408-3 PDF

Dwight S. M. Mutonono has asserted his right under the Copyright, Designs and Patents Act, 1988 to be identified as the Author of this work.

All rights reserved. No part of this publication may be reproduced, stored in a retrieval system or transmitted, in any form or by any means, electronic, mechanical, photocopying, recording or otherwise, without the prior written permission of the publisher or the Copyright Licensing Agency.

All Scripture quotations, unless otherwise indicated, are taken from The Holy Bible, New International Version®, NIV® Copyright © 1973, 1978, 1984, 2011 by Biblica, Inc.® Used by permission. All rights reserved worldwide.

British Library Cataloguing in Publication Data
A catalogue record for this book is available from the British Library

ISBN: 978-1-78368-405-2

Cover design: projectluz.com
Book design: To a Tee Ltd, www.2at.com

The publishers of this book actively supports theological dialogue and an author's right to publish but does not necessarily endorse the views and opinions set forth here or in works referenced within this publication, nor can we guarantee technical and grammatical correctness. The publishers do not accept any responsibility or liability to persons or property as a consequence of the reading, use or interpretation of its published content.

In memory of my dad, Moses Nyamadzawo Mutonono, an artist and author but most of all a model leader and father

CONTENTS

Foreword: Resurrecting the African Spirit ix
Acknowledgements xv

1 Introduction 1
2 Africa's Indignity 5
3 Joseph's Leadership and Stewardship 9
4 Jonah's Failure as a Steward 31
5 Forgiveness and Reconciliation 41
6 Morality and Integrity 63
7 Stewardship and Power 83
8 Governance and Conflict Transformation 105
9 Restoring Africa's Dignity 121

Bibliography 125

FOREWORD

RESURRECTING THE AFRICAN SPIRIT

I couldn't stop the tears that started flowing down my face. I couldn't understand why I was crying either. Gradually, I came to realize that I was mourning the death of the African spirit and wrestling with God on what could be done about it.

The year was 1995 and the place was a lecture theatre at Yensel University in Seoul, South Korea. I was amongst a group of fifty African leaders invited to experience the prayer movement that was fuelling the missionary endeavour from that country. During our visit, we were shown a movie of former students returning to say thank you to the university for what it had invested in them. These men and women were now leaders in various fields of Korean society. The pride they displayed in their university and country shook me to the core. I was confronted with a spirit that I knew I did not have as an African.

When Zimbabwe became independent in 1980, we had all sorts of dreams about our future under an African leader. Our graduating class of 1980 was given the option of having either "University of Rhodesia" or "University of Zimbabwe" on our certificates. It's not difficult to guess why we chose "University of Zimbabwe". We were so hopeful! Fifteen years into our independence, I regretted that decision. Sitting in that lecture theatre, I realized I was not proud of my university in the same way that those Koreans were proud of theirs. Corruption had weakened the integrity of our qualifications.

Not only was I not proud of my university, I was also embarrassed to be a Zimbabwean, and for that matter an African. Customs authorities around the world not only searched our suitcases but also wanted to search our stomachs because some of us were ingesting drugs to smuggle them. I was embarrassed to be a black man because of all that we were then known for. Those with options were leaving the continent to carve out futures elsewhere. Something had died inside of us and needed resurrecting.

Through my tears and meditations in the days that followed, seven simple words emerged that have given me hope that Africa can be changed.

Identity. The slave trade and colonial rule so eroded our identity that we wanted to be copycats and look like our masters. Massive identity theft left us without a clue about who we were, where we had come from, and consequently, where we were going. Without a clear sense of identity, you are nobody. Others speak and decide for you. Africa produced one of the earliest civilizations, nursed the birth of the Jewish race, and protected the birth of Christianity both in the form of baby Jesus and later in AD 70 when Jerusalem was destroyed by the Romans. No wonder the church in Africa is mushrooming; the gospel is simply coming back home!

Principled Leadership. African leadership for the most part, lacks principle. I would argue that our problems are not rooted in flawed constitutions or a lack of democracy or rigged elections. They are rooted in our value systems, our lack of clear dreams of where we are going and how we are going to get there. They are rooted in the hearts of our leaders whose promises are not worth the paper they are written on, promises that are broken before the victory celebrations end. At the risk of being stoned, I sometimes wonder whether Africans are ready for democratic governance. Would we be better served by chieftainship in some form of mature, benevolent dictatorship? For the most part, democratic rule in Africa is a thin veneer beneath which lies a network of entitlement and sycophancy that masks corruption and violence. Until we lead from principle rather than personal preference, we are doomed to the merry-go-round that we find ourselves on.

Responsibility. Knowing who we are and being fuelled by principle will lead to our taking responsibility for our destiny. We've played the blame game for long enough. You can be killed on our streets while people are watching. The actions of the two men who were stabbed to death for defending a Muslim girl in the United States sound like foolishness to most Africans. Have you ever wondered why the paths in our villages meander like rivers? For a long time, I wrestled with God on this. Why had he not given Africans scientific minds that realized that the shortest distance between two points was a straight line? The answer came when I discovered that the paths start out straight, but then a tree falls on the path, or a mound grows, or an animal dies and the smell forces people to take a detour. Nobody thinks to remove the obstruction. Instead, we find an alternative route, and before long the path resembles a snake. It's the same reason we put up with bad leadership; it's too risky to raise our voices. It's time for us to come to terms with the fact that the buck stops at our door. We are responsible for what happens around us.

Stewardship. Until we realize that we are stewards and not owners, we will continue to abuse the power that has been entrusted to us as leaders. In most African governments, public assets have been privatized. The army, the police and even the judiciary now exist to protect the men in power and not the civilians who elected them. Sad to say, give most Africans a house, and before long it will be falling to pieces. You dare not loan your car to most Africans; it will come back with an empty tank or worse still, with some concealed fault. Give an African a country, and look at what we've done with the continent! We have often failed to improve on what we inherited.

Accountability. Leaders are civil servants who must give an account of their stewardship. Elections are meant to be an opportunity for them to show what they have done with the power entrusted to them. Sadly, the word "accountability" does not even exist in most African languages. When I've used this word in contexts where I was speaking through an interpreter, the poor guy had to take time to explain the concept. Chiefs were usually not accountable to those they led, and you dared not challenge them. African leaders must be made accountable for their stewardship through a system of checks and balances. Opposition must not be stifled, and holding a different view must not be condemned as treason.

Creativity was my sixth word to resurrect the African spirit. Somehow, Africans think that the solution to our problems will come in a briefcase with someone from outside. Yet in most instances, the solution is so obvious you wonder why we have failed to use our own common sense. Diseases that used to kill Westerners have been almost totally eradicated, and yet they are still rampant in Africa today. African leadership discourages thinkers, frowns on experimentation, and thrives on what worked in yesteryear. When our children ask why the sky is blue, we think they are being a nuisance and shut them up. We fail to understand that questioning why things are the way they are leads to improvement. We send our children to the best schools in the West and yet fail to create an enabling environment for them to return to. Consequently, when they finish, they stay abroad. People talk of the African brain drain, I think we should talk of it as a haemorrhage! We have lost most of our best brains, with the West being the beneficiaries. The solutions to our problems lie within us. Until we release creativity, we will continue to languish in poverty, disease and underdevelopment.

Discipline. Discipline in daily routines, knowing when to wake up and when to sleep, discipline to work hard at honest work to gain honest profit. Our people believe in miracle cures. That's why we are so gullible that we will believe in miracle money, drink diesel and eat grass and be exploited by unscrupulous religious charlatans. We have no sense of the value of time. We boast that Westerners have watches but we have time, and we fail to realize that a minute in the West is the same as a minute in Africa. In this networked global economy, if we do not use our time wisely, we will be left in the dust. Africans must learn the discipline of delayed gratification. Blessed are you, oh land, when your princes feast for strength and not for pleasure. We must learn the discipline of due process. I've yet to find anyone who had a ten-year-old in less than ten years!

I first met Dwight when he and his friends started coming to our church as high-school students. From then on, I have been privileged to walk alongside him as he has developed as a leader. Sensing a call to ministry, he would have walked straight into church work after high school, but we encouraged him to find a job in the marketplace. His training as an air traffic controller instilled in him certain disciplines that have yielded fruit in his ministry. We didn't influence his choice of a spouse, but I was privileged to join them in matrimony. At some point, he would have become the senior pastor of our family of churches, but we encouraged him to take the academic path that eventually led to his appointment as Director of the Africa Leadership and Management Academy. Today, he is one of our leading academic brains and theological watchmen.

I can wholeheartedly say that Dwight is a son who carries the genes of the message above. The book you hold in your hands is his second effort to describe the style of leadership we have striven to model. I look forward to more books from this man before this journey is over. I hope you find this one as provoking, challenging and yet refreshing as I have found my interaction with him.

Enjoy.

Ngwiza Mnkandla
Bishop, Faith Ministries Churches
Zimbabwe

ACKNOWLEDGEMENTS

This book is the result of collaboration with several people whom I would like to acknowledge. Without them, you probably would not be holding the book you have in your hands. They have been a big part of my development, and a silent part of them is in every word that you read.

First, I would like to thank Langham Partnership for affording me the opportunity to be published in this way. When I first submitted my manuscript to them, I thought I had given them an almost perfect document. They graciously agreed to publish it after giving it to peer reviewers, who scrutinized and took it apart sentence by sentence. I had questions to answer and corrections to make. Then I and the Langham team made several revisions to get the book to the level where it could be published. This has been a learning process for me, and I am humbled to see what they have helped my book to become. I would like to specifically mention Peter Fleck, Isobel Stevenson, Pieter Kwant, Vivian Doub, Dahlia Fraser and Luke Lewis as some of the people who helped make this happen.

Second, I would like to thank some men and women who have played a great part in the spiritual development of myself and my wife. Pastor (now Bishop, a title that he knows I don't like) Ngwiza and Maureen Mnkandla have been a part of our lives since 1982. They have nurtured us through the years and have been instrumental in our development as leaders. Pastor Mike and Cheryth Andre, who are now in Canada, played a significant role in our early Christian growth. We planted a church with them in the early nineteen eighties. Nick Bewes, the Bible School principal, helped to sharpen my biblical thinking and anchor me in the faith. Rodney and Cortina Orr helped me to become a more refined academic by introducing me to Africa Leadership and Management Academy (ALMA). Rodney, together with Mike Wicker supervised my Masters dissertation and convinced me to work with ALMA, a life-changing experience that has opened many doors that I would otherwise probably not have walked through. Faith Ministries released and supported me in 2003 to work with ALMA, which is a school that is run by a missionary organization. Through ALMA I met Tokunboh Adeyemo and was privileged to contribute an article for the *Africa Bible Commentary*. That's how I first interacted with Langham Partnership, who helped publish that commentary. Lately I have been working with Delanyo Adadevoh, a man whose heart for Africa and whose writings and thinking have been a great source of inspiration for me.

Third, through the years, many friends have come alongside us as Christian leaders and helped us along the way. They include Shingi and Wilma Munyeza, Farai and Chipo Katsande, Ken and Pam Chitenhe, Mike and Angie Holland, Rob and Zodwa Makombe, Tendai and Theresa Mafunda, Doug and Tendai Mamvura, Phibion and Mary Gwatidzo, Matthew and Priscilla Wazara, Anthony and Sibonile Chinhara, Ronald and Ruvimbo Marikano, Brockton Hefflin, Lungisani and Kuda Ncube who pastor our congregation, and my big brother Kevin Musarira.

Some young friends we have been working with recently are close to my heart, and are sharpening and challenging us as a couple. They include Ian and Sandra Muringayi, Nolan and Violet Kahonde, Thomas and Monica Matikiti.

Finally, I would like to thank my wife, my helpmeet, Martha, who has been used by God to shape me as a man. Our children Tinotenda and Unopa have been a great blessing to us. We pray that they will catch a vision to transform Africa in their generation. Not forgetting Blessing Tsodzo, Nonkululeko and Kyansambo Vundla, our foster children whom God gave us in the nineteen nineties.

When the Apostle Paul wrote to the Philippians, he said "finally" twice, and so, finally, I would like to thank Martha's and my remaining parents. Martha's mom is a great inspiration to us all (and especially to our son, Unopa). My mother continues to be my hero. Along with my dad she has been a pillar of strength for me.

1

INTRODUCTION

I am a Zimbabwean and an African. Whenever I leave my country, I am made to feel that this is something I should be ashamed of. The condition of my country has become the joke of the world; mention Zimbabwe and many laugh. We are the subjects of global comedy. Whether I am in China, the United Kingdom or the United States, I encounter the same attitudes and negative perceptions and hear snide remarks about African political leaders. Those who are polite and fear being called racist withhold sharp comments that they would otherwise make, but the truth is they are acutely aware of glaring leadership failures in all spheres of African society.

How do I respond to these criticisms? I know that our African leaders have made great positive contributions that are often ignored, but I cannot deny that Africa has deep social, economic, political and religious problems. Some would blame all these on our colonial past, but other parts of the world that also endured colonial domination and gained their independence at much the same time as African countries have surged ahead economically, and their citizens are far better off. Yet while I see these problems, and endure the "indignity" of being called a Zimbabwean and an African, I am not ashamed of my heritage. I see myself as having been given a unique opportunity to speak to my generation about what could be and to challenge Africans to become all that God intended.

Centuries ago, great African thinkers like Cyprian, Tertullian, Origen and Augustine helped shape Christianity as we know it. Africans played a crucial role in the development of the faith. And Africa is now poised to regain that role. The demographics of church growth over the past one hundred years are clear. Africa has become a centre of world Christianity. Philip Jenkins claims that by 2025 Africa and South America will have the highest concentration of Christians on the globe.

You may think that I am a hopeless optimist to think that the African church can transform the African continent, let alone world Christianity. But such transformation is not without precedent. Five hundred years ago who would have expected that the actions of an obscure monk in a small state in Germany would launch the Protestant Reformation that transformed European society? Who would have expected that the preaching of John Calvin in Geneva would ultimately affect the newly discovered American continent? Or that the work of one man, William Wilberforce, would bring an end to the international slave trade? God used these people, and men like John Wesley, to start Christian movements that changed whole societies. Christianity got out of the church building and permeated society. Why should something similar not happen in Africa today?

Going back even further in history, we know that the church played a large role in transforming the society of ancient Rome and that the monastic movement transformed Europe and led over time to the end of many barbaric practices. This is what happens when Christianity becomes dominant in any given region. One expects to see the growth of the faith accompanied by rising integrity, better stewardship and good governance. While Christianity has caused bloody and destructive conflicts and Christian leaders have had many human imperfections, Christianity's overall contribution to society has generally resulted in higher moral and governance standards.

Yet we are not seeing this in Africa. While the number of those who say they are Christians is rising, Africa does not look like a continent that is predominantly Christian. This book is an appeal to the African church to rise up and lead godly transformation on this continent.

I will begin by outlining what I call the lack of dignity in the Zimbabwean and African condition. Then I will draw lessons from the life of someone who also experienced suffering and indignity but grew to become a great leader. The story of Joseph in the book of Genesis provides many lessons about forgiveness and reconciliation, morality and integrity, stewardship, governance and conflict transformation. Joseph is a good example of how to use God-given power in the service of others.

Then we will turn to look at Jonah, someone whose attitude is very different from that of Joseph as regards forgiveness, reconciliation and compassion, but who was also used by God and was taught valuable lessons about leadership.

Finally, we will see how what we have learned from Joseph and Jonah applies to leadership in Africa. We will focus on forgiveness and reconciliation, morality and integrity, stewardship, governance and conflict transformation as ways in which the African church can spearhead the positive transformation of the continent.

2

AFRICA'S INDIGNITY

The late Professor Ali Mazrui, a respected Kenyan Islamic academic and writer, once described Africa as a retarded continent, saying, "In world affairs the continent does not act as a unit; on the contrary, it is subject to the weakness of its national, ethnic, ideological and religious cleavages."

Although Ali Mazrui and I do not agree on matters of faith, I respect his thinking and I believe that God gives gifts of leadership to both Christians and non-Christians. However, in my opinion the greatest leadership thinking is that which comes from God, the creator of heaven and earth, and mature Christians who have learned leadership principles from his word make the greatest leaders. It is possible to have the principles of Christ without the person of Christ, but to have both the person and principles is preferable. Ali Mazrui is an example of a man who has understood the principles but perhaps not the person of Christ.

Mazrui's description is accepted. Africa is like a child who is failing to reach the expected developmental goals. The late Tokunboh Adeyemo recognized this, for he too battled with what he called the African enigma: "An enigma is a puzzling thing or person. It is a riddle or a paradox. It is something hard to explain and difficult to understand." Adeyemo pointed to the enigma that Africa is the richest continent in the world, yet has the poorest people in the world. While African professionals and executives are making many nations rich, their own nations and continent remain the poorest in the world. While these émigrés enjoy affluence and prosperity, their villages of origin are in a pitiful state.

It is easy to point fingers at those who leave and make other nations rich, but there is also an enigma when it comes to those who stay. What kind of a people are we when we use leadership positions to enrich ourselves, and in the process impoverish those who have chosen us to lead them? Dambisa Moyo is puzzled when she compares African leaders to Asian leaders. Asian leaders are just as corrupt if not more corrupt than African leaders, yet Asian corruption is positive corruption because these leaders at least invest their ill-gotten wealth in their own countries, thereby helping their economies and providing jobs for the poor. African leaders, on the other hand, steal from their people and invest the wealth in Europe and in Western banks. Vast amounts of African money stolen by African leaders is found in Europe.

We saw evidence of this in the Arab uprisings in North Africa as news poured out about the vast sums the leaders had stashed away in European institutions. It was concerning that the Europeans only froze the bank accounts when they realized the African leaders were in trouble and might want to withdraw their money. All of a sudden it was recognized that the leaders were despotic and accumulating funds illegitimately, and that they were going to use these funds to further oppress their people. Therefore the funds were frozen. It seems that as far as the Europeans were concerned, these leaders were good people when they put money in their banks, but became evil around the time they wanted to get it out.

Acemoglu and Robinson allege that Hosni Mubarak of Egypt had accumulated $70 billion dollars; an incredible amount, particularly when you consider that Zimbabwe's gross domestic product is currently between $10 and $12 billion. And Mubarak's alleged privatization of huge sums of public funds is not unique. Arab leaders like the late Muammar Gaddafi and deposed Tunisian leader Zine El Abidine Ben Ali were alleged to have vast amounts stashed in overseas foreign accounts. Nor does this happen only in North Africa. Sub-Saharan leaders like the late leader Mobutu Sese Seko of Congo (which he renamed Zaire) and Sani Abacha of Nigeria were known to have huge stashes of money in Swiss banks. Much of this money has never returned to Africa. Yahya Jammeh, the former president of Gambia, has been accused of stealing $50 million before leaving for exile in Equatorial Guinea. How much he plundered during his twenty-two-year rule is still the subject of investigation. But Dambisa Moyo says that as much as a trillion dollars have departed Africa over the past fifty years through privatization of public funds.

It is not only money that leaks out of Africa. A huge volume of natural resources also leave the continent as raw minerals that have been "privatized". According to Valerie Noury, "The untapped mineral wealth of DR Congo is estimated at $24 trillion, equivalent to the GDP of Europe and the United States combined; making Congo potentially the richest country in the world. It eclipses even the $18 trillion total value of Saudi Arabia's oil reserves." She cites a United Nations report that says that the mineral called coltan is leaving the DRC in huge quantities, largely unaccounted for, benefiting the Rwandan Patriotic Army and also enriching top Ugandan military commanders and civilians. As evidence she cites the fact that in 2000 "Rwanda produced 83 tons of coltan from its own mines, yet nevertheless managed to export 603 tons!" Only in Africa can you export more than you produce, and no one asks questions. All this is happening on the backs of Congolese workers, who on average earn only US$10 a month.

Finally, Zimbabwe so mismanaged its economy that it eventually abolished the Zimbabwean dollar after inflation reached world record levels, second only to what had happened in Hungary in 1946. The inflation rate was 13.2 billion percent per month, or 516 quintillion percent per year and the highest denominated note was a 100 trillion dollar bill that is now valued at forty US cents.

The indignity of Africa is that while many people live in some of the most appalling conditions in the world, those in social, economic and political power are only interested in enriching themselves. They enjoy Hollywood lifestyles while surrounded by poverty and misery.

The African story needs to change, and change will come when biblically informed leaders rise up and give leadership that uses God-given resources for the benefit of all. Such leaders are stewards, fit to be entrusted with the resources of others. They operate like Joseph did when he became a high official in Egypt. He did not use the fact that he had started out poor as an excuse for greed, nor did he allow the fact that he had been exploited to justify exploitation of others.

We will be looking at his story in more detail before we go on to consider how African Christians can engage African society as steward leaders who will use the resources God gives us for the benefit of all.

For Discussion

The following questions relate to issues that will be discussed at more length in this book, but you would do well to think about your own answers to them before you read further.

1. What would you say to someone who says that Christians should concern themselves only with church-related activities like praying, singing hymns, preaching and the like, and leave politics to politicians and business to business people?
2. What does Christianity have to do with the running of nations, their wealth or poverty, the dignity of a people, and the positive transformation of societies?
3. How, if at all, does making disciples translate to making societal leaders?
4. Before a person deals with the macro problems that affect entire countries, it is necessary to deal with the microenvironment of his or her own life. What should a person do in his or her personal life, home, neighbourhood, or community to bring personal change?

3

JOSEPH'S LEADERSHIP AND STEWARDSHIP

Joseph first appears in the biblical record in Genesis 37, where he is introduced as a young man growing up in a family with ten older brothers and one younger brother. The number of sisters is not mentioned, but we do know from Genesis 34 that he had at least one. I would recommend that you reread the story in Genesis 37–50 before reading the rest of this chapter.

Joseph's Background

Families determine the quality of persons released into wider society, and so it is important to know something of Joseph's family. He was the great-grandson of Abraham, through whom God had promised to raise up a nation that would be uniquely his own. The family lived with a consciousness that they served the one true God, creator of heaven and earth, and that they were to be his representatives in the world.

After the events at the Tower of Babel, God had dispersed people across the earth. Then he chose to focus his attention on one man, Abraham, and his descendants. Through this man God was going to start a nation through whom he would communicate to the rest of the world. This nation would be a special group of people with whom he would intimately relate and who would understand his ways. Adadevoh describes God's purpose in choosing Israel like this:

God's purpose in choosing Israel was to establish it on godly principles as an example for other nations. The nations will observe:
- The righteous decrees and laws of Israel.
- The wisdom and understanding of the people of Israel.
- The closeness to God of the people of Israel, demonstrated through answered prayers.

In this way the nation of Israel was meant to be a light to other nations. Being a light means a nation is governed by righteous decrees, the citizens are filled with knowledge, wisdom and understanding, and God is supernaturally showering his blessings on the nation.[1]

Abraham's son Isaac and then his grandson Jacob, who was renamed Israel, became the custodians of the nation that God was establishing. Yet even though Jacob was the grandson of Abraham and the leader of the chosen people, life in his family was far from ideal. His uncle Laban tricked him into marrying two sisters. Jacob's love and preference for Rachel was like petrol poured on the fire of sibling rivalry. Leah and Rachel competed for Jacob's attention, trying to outdo each other in giving him children. They even resorted to giving him their personal servants to have children with. By the time we get to Genesis 37, Jacob had twelve sons by four women. These sons eventually became the heads of the twelve tribes of Israel.

Forgiveness and Reconciliation

Although chosen by God, Jacob's family was deeply flawed. They offer a microcosm of the issues that all nations face in one form or another, including historical pain, forgiveness and reconciliation.

Joseph's pain

Jacob was not wise in that he did nothing about the sibling rivalry between his two wives and fanned the sibling rivalry among his offspring

---

[1] Delanyo Adadevoh, *The Whole Gospel to the Whole Person* (Orlando, FL: International Leadership Foundation, 2012), 31–32.

by giving preferential treatment to Joseph and Benjamin, the children of his favourite wife, Rachel. These two were also the youngest of the twelve brothers.

The first time we meet Joseph he is giving a bad report to his father Jacob (or Israel as he is called in the text) about his brothers, and Jacob is showing his special love for him by giving him a special robe. We do not know exactly what made this robe special; it may have been multi-coloured, or decorated with embroidery, or woven of special wool, or have had long sleeves. These details do not matter; what makes this gift significant is the message it sent: Joseph was the favourite, and as such he was "not expected to do heavy work; he was the chosen heir to rule over the family". No wonder Joseph's brothers were jealous and envied Joseph – and envy is a very dangerous emotion. The resentment it feeds can easily result in aggression and physical harm to the person perceived as more gifted or privileged.

Not only was Joseph given preferential treatment by his father, he also ingratiated himself with his father by bringing a bad report about his brothers. Whether the report was true is secondary to his motivation in bringing it. Was Joseph taking malicious pleasure in getting his brothers into trouble, or was he merely informing his father about some things he ought to know? We are not told, but the older brothers were not pleased that their younger brother had snitched on them. They saw his action as a betrayal, a breach of brotherly etiquette, and had all the more reason to resent him.

The tension in Jacob's home must have been palpable. The division between their mothers was the source of and fuelled the divisions between the brothers. The children probably never fully understood the depth of the conflict they were involved in since its origins predated them; they were just born into it.

At seventeen Joseph was probably aware of the divisions in his family, but he may have been childishly naïve about the extent of his brothers' hatred of him. When he told them his dreams, did he not know the effect this would have on them? If he did not know the first time, he probably knew the second time, and yet he told them his dream anyway.

The conflict in the home continued to escalate until one day it boiled over and became violent. The brothers seriously considered murdering Joseph. Had they done so, they would have been guilty of fratricide (brother killing brother), a particularly appalling type of murder. Brothers should look out for and protect each other; when brother kills brother it is evidence of very broken and fallen relationships. Clearly the relationships in Jacob's family were far from the godly ideal befitting a family that was supposed to represent God to the world.

Eventually Judah convinced his brothers not to kill Joseph: "What will we gain if we kill our brother and cover up his blood? Come, let's sell him to the Ishmaelites and not lay our hands on him; after all, he is our brother, our own flesh and blood" (Gen 37:26–27). Rather than killing him, they would sell him as a slave.

Joseph, thrown into a pit, probably heard his brothers discuss the possibility of killing him. If he had not known the depth of their hatred of him before, now he did. The experience of being pulled out of the pit and seeing traders handing over twenty pieces of silver to buy him must have been etched in his memory. He would have begged his brothers not to sell him into slavery. He must have wept, but they ignored his pleas (Gen 42:21). This was his last memory of his brothers. He would not see them again for twenty-two years. (Genesis 41:46 says Joseph was thirty years old when he entered the service of Pharaoh, and he saw his brothers two years into the famine that he prophesied would come after the seven years of plenty (Gen 45:6). Consequently, if Joseph was seventeen when his brothers sold him, he was about thirty-nine years old when he next saw them.) The traumatic parting from his brothers would have been a painful memory and perhaps even a recurring nightmare.

Joseph's troubles were just beginning. He would go on to encounter huge injustice in Potiphar's household. He worked hard for Potiphar and was so outstanding in his work that Potiphar gave him charge over all he had. But Potiphar had a corrupt wife who thought she could corrupt Joseph.

Joseph had too high a character to be drawn into sexual immorality. When Mrs Potiphar tried to seduce him, he ran away, leaving his coat in her hands. She was so angered by Joseph's refusing her advances that she accused him of attempting to rape her. But she was the one who had attempted to rape him! Joseph was slandered. He must have endured an emotional battering, besides any physical beating that Potiphar or the servants gave him.

Joseph had fallen from being the favourite child in his father's house, and possibly even the chosen heir, to being a slave. Potiphar's wife took him a step lower: not only was he a slave, he was now a convicted criminal. We could understand Joseph's becoming deeply angry and embittered. The law of reciprocity (do good to those who are good to you and hit back at those who harm you) that most people live by would make him want to cry out for vengeance for the injustices he had suffered. Images of his brothers selling him into slavery and Mrs Potiphar sending him to prison must have haunted him. His words to his prison mate, the cupbearer whose dream he interpreted, are testimony to the fact that he felt victimized:

> When all goes well with you, remember me and show me kindness; mention me to Pharaoh and get me out of this prison. I was forcibly carried off from the land of the Hebrews, and even here I have done nothing to deserve being put in a dungeon. (Gen 40:15)

He hoped that somehow he would eventually find justice through the social systems of the time, for a cupbearer was a very important person. He was the manager of Pharaoh's personal affairs, responsible for ensuring that no harm, especially by poisoning, came to Pharaoh. Joseph hoped that this man would be kind enough to mention his case to Pharaoh at the appropriate time. This did not happen as quickly as he must have hoped, for he languished in prison for two more years.

That time in prison must have been soul-destroying. Joseph must have felt rejected, abandoned and forgotten by the world. Amazingly he remained steadfast in faith; in fact the recurring statement in the midst of all the troubles mentioned in Genesis 39 is "the Lord was with Joseph". Somehow Joseph managed to hold on even though everything around him fell apart and did not make sense. We could understand if Joseph had wanted to "curse God and die" as Job's wife advised (Job 2:9). But like Job, Joseph's relationship with God was so deep and intimate that he found God to be the only sure thing in the midst of all the turmoil of his life.

Joseph's comfort

The years in prison must have been very difficult for Joseph. Yet he could find rest in the Lord. The Lord was with him. Those who have walked with God through trials and temptations of any kind will know the precious lessons about trusting God that are learned at such times.

Joseph's comfort began in his spirit. He was intimately in touch with God's Spirit, whom the Apostle John refers to as the Comforter. Easton's Bible Dictionary has this to say about that word:

> *Comforter*: the designation of the Holy Ghost (John 14:16, 26; 15:26; 16:7; R. V. marg., "or Advocate, or Helper; Gr. *paracletos*"). The same Greek word thus rendered is translated "Advocate" in 1 John 2:1 as applicable to Christ. It means properly "one who is summoned to the side of another" to help him in a court of justice by defending him, "one who is summoned to plead a cause." "Advocate" is the proper rendering of the word in every case where it occurs.[2]

Joseph cried out for a human advocate, but God himself was his advocate. The greatest comfort for the righteous is that there is a God in heaven who sees and knows everything. Only those who have learned to dwell "in the shelter of the Most High" (Ps 91:1) know the powerful significance of that reality.

At some point when God saw that Joseph was ready to walk into the full extent of his life's calling, he gave a dream to Pharaoh and reminded the cupbearer of Joseph. As a result, Joseph suddenly found himself elevated to a position of leadership. Such a jump in status would have affected even the strongest of people and would definitely make for pride. Only a truly broken person with a sober understanding of life such as Joseph had gained would survive such exaltation and not let it go to his head.

> So Pharaoh said to Joseph, "I hereby put you in charge of the whole land of Egypt." Then Pharaoh took his signet ring from his finger and put it on Joseph's finger. He dressed him in robes of fine linen and put a gold chain around his neck.

---

[2] M. G. Easton, *Illustrated Bible Dictionary* (New York: Cosimo Classics, 2006).

> He had him ride in a chariot as his second-in-command, and people shouted before him, "Make way!" Thus he put him in charge of the whole land of Egypt.
>
> Then Pharaoh said to Joseph, "I am Pharaoh, but without your word no one will lift hand or foot in all Egypt." (Gen 41:41–44)

Having the king's signet ring or seal was equivalent to having full signing rights or power of attorney over all Pharaoh had. Such power would feed one's ego, and most people would become big-headed, but God had prepared Joseph for it. He would remember the fate of the baker and the cupbearer and know how whimsical and capricious Pharaoh could be. Pharaoh was like God in that land; justice started and ended with him, and whatever he said stood. But it was ultimately God who had exalted Joseph, a man whose worldview was firmly rooted in the reality of the one true God, creator of heaven and earth, sovereign over all human affairs.

Joseph married the daughter of an Egyptian priest of On (this marriage will be discussed in the section on Joseph's morality and integrity). For now, however, it is enough to note that the name of his first son, Manasseh means "to forget". He gave his son that name saying, "God has made me forget all my trouble and all my father's household" (Gen 41:51). It seems the joy of having a wife and children, as well as the privileges he enjoyed in Egypt, soothed Joseph's emotional pain.

From great humiliation, Joseph rose to great honour. Within a single day, the shame and humiliation that came from becoming a slave and a prisoner were replaced with the honour of occupying the second highest office in the land, second only to Pharaoh. The suddenness of the transition must have been mind-blowing!

The Bible does not mention how Mrs Potiphar reacted to the news of Joseph's appointment; I would love to have seen her face! God vindicated Joseph in a big way, far beyond what he could possibly have asked for. So great was God's vindication of Joseph that I, a Zimbabwean, am still writing about the events that took place in his life some four thousand years ago. If Mrs Potiphar knew that her story would be told to the whole world for thousands of years to come, she might have thought twice about what she was doing. If Joseph's brothers had known the significance of what they did to Joseph and how the story would be told, they too might have behaved differently. They thought that what they did was in secret, but now it is being shouted from the rooftops. They thought they had squashed Joseph for good, using their power over him to inflict maximum pain, but they did not know that one day God would vindicate him and the truth would come out. Joseph was comforted and justice was done, perhaps not in the way he envisaged, but in a much better way than he could ever have dreamed of.

God the perfect Advocate and Judge is our refuge in times of need. Joseph learned that lesson, and so must all leaders who desire to be effective for God.

Joseph's kindness

Yet another incredible aspect of this story comes when Joseph finally reconnects with his brothers after about twenty-two years. He immediately recognized them, but they did not recognize him. This is understandable; facial features can change considerably from teenage years to full adulthood, and Joseph was speaking Egyptian, a language foreign to them. The thought that Joseph might have risen to be second-in-command in Egypt would be beyond their wildest imagining; after all he was not even an Egyptian. They thought they were talking to an Egyptian man who held the rank of a vizier. This was a powerful position – somewhat like the office of prime minister in the United Kingdom. The language he used, his regalia and the power of his office all made it difficult for the brothers to see that the man standing in front of them was their brother Joseph.

When Joseph's brothers bowed down to him with their faces to the ground, he remembered his prophetic dreams about them (Gen 42:6–9). Then he spoke to them roughly, accusing them of being spies. Was Joseph using the reversal of circumstances to torment his brothers as they had tormented him? Was he trying to make them feel emotional pain in revenge for what they had put him through? Was he enjoying the prospect of making them stew and suffer?

As the story develops, we see that rather than tormenting them, Joseph was testing them. The test was designed to assess the condition of their hearts. Had they changed at all in the past twenty-two years?

Joseph's deep affection for his brothers is revealed in the many times that he turned away to weep as he heard them talking remorsefully about what they had done to him. It seems that he wanted to discern their hearts before knowing how to relate with them. The scales of power had shifted in Joseph's favour. Even if they wanted to, the brothers could do him no harm. He, however, could now do what he wanted with them, and he had all the state machinery of Egypt at his disposal to use as he wished, justly or unjustly, for good or for evil, to oppress or to release. Joseph wanted to see how his brothers were now using power in order to know how best to use his own power.

Joseph knew from personal experience how heartless and cruel his brothers could be. He knew the divisions in his family. During the many years he had spent apart from them, he must have wondered about those closest to his heart, the two men who were not involved in this conspiracy against him, his father and his brother Benjamin. Had his brothers harmed them? What was the extent of their culpability in doing harm to others? Had it stopped with him or had it gone further? The answers to those questions would determine what he would do and how he would relate to them. He was determined not to use his power to settle personal scores but for the benefit of those who were weak and oppressed. In this instance, it was for his elderly father and younger brother that he was most concerned.

He would also have been interested in observing the level of friction between the brothers. Were they still so divided that they could not meaningfully work together? Were they still murderous people capable of fratricide, or had they changed? His love for them was indubitable and his behaviour towards them was not malicious. But he was not sentimental. He was measured, cautious and calculating. His love was not just affectionate; it was God's kind of love, a love that is motivated by the will and not just by emotion; a love that is given freely to all but which requires a response of faith and obedience to his commands.

Ultimately Joseph wanted to know whether his brothers had enough godly character in them to be worthy representatives of him. To Joseph's great joy, he found that the brothers were truly remorseful, even repentant. He saw their great concern for Jacob and Benjamin, to the extent of even being prepared to die for them. They had indeed changed. The years had broken these hard men. God's dealings with them and their feelings of guilt and remorse were evident. They had undergone a heart transformation. They passed Joseph's numerous tests, and eventually Joseph revealed himself to them.

The moment of Joseph's self-revelation to his brothers must have struck fear into them. The biblical record says that he wept so loudly that the Egyptians who were outside and even Pharaoh's household heard it. The sight and sound of a grown man breaking down and weeping like that is alarming. All the years of pent-up emotion were pouring out of Joseph. And when the brothers grasped who the Egyptian vizier actually was, they were dumbfounded. They suddenly realized the extent of his power over them. They were at his mercy, and here he was, a grown man crying so loudly that everyone within hearing distance could hear him weep.

The words of reassurance that Joseph spoke were key. There was no hint of malice in them: "I am your brother Joseph, the one you sold into Egypt! And now, do not be distressed and do not be angry with yourselves for selling me here, because it was to save lives that God sent me ahead of you" (Gen 45:4–5).

Joseph's reconciliation with his brothers came out of a realization that ultimately the sovereign hand of God was behind all the pain he had endured. He had wrestled with God over this matter until he finally saw events from God's sovereign perspective. Yes, his brothers were cruel, even demonically influenced, but once he saw events from God's perspective, the brothers' actions became what they really were, the foolish actions of ignorant, uninformed individuals. They were to be pitied rather than punished. Joseph would have understood Jesus' words on the cross: "Forgive them, for they do not know what they are doing" (Luke 23:34).

In this book, the process through which Joseph reached the point where he could see God's hand in all that happened is referred to as conflict transformation. It will be discussed at length in later chapters.

Joseph's Morality and Integrity

Joseph's character is a consistent thread throughout this story. From the moment he first appears on the scene, he is unquestionably committed to God. Even his tendency to give bad reports about his brothers indicates that he had high moral values and took exception to bad behaviour. He was what children would term a "goody-goody", always doing what he should. The problem with goody-goodies is that they often make themselves look good by showing how bad others are. Perhaps this is the only way that Joseph could be faulted.

His conduct in Potiphar's house was so outstanding that Potiphar entrusted him with everything he owned. Not even the allure of Mrs Potiphar could derail him. Even in prison, his code of conduct was so high that he was put in charge of all the other prisoners. It seems that wherever Joseph went, he ended up in charge, greatly trusted by the authorities. What was it that made Joseph so attractive? A big part of it was his morality and integrity.

Joseph was correctly aligned with God. We can see his awareness of God in his response to Mrs Potiphar: "How then could I do such a wicked thing and sin against God?" (Gen 39:10). He was conscious that his daily actions were done in the sight of God, and he conducted himself as a person who was living before an audience of one.

Joseph's integrity was tested in many ways. His moral fortitude was put to the test when he was entrusted with positions of responsibility and by the behaviour of Mrs Potiphar. The integrity of his faith in God and what God had revealed through dreams was tested. The trials he went through would have derailed the faith of many, but Joseph stood firm:

> He [God] called down famine on the land
> and destroyed all their supplies of food;
> and he sent a man before them
> Joseph, sold as a slave.
> They bruised his feet with shackles,
> his neck was put in irons
> till what he foretold came to pass,
> till the word of the LORD proved him true. (Ps 105:16–19)

Joseph was regularly entrusted with new responsibilities because human leaders saw his godly character and recognized that it would be logical to trust him. Even God judged him worthy of being entrusted with the task of saving his people. Though his dreams came in the early part of his life, before he went through the tough process of enslavement and imprisonment, the process was the preparation and test; only after the test was he entrusted with the fulfilment of his dreams.

Integrity in Pharaoh's court

When Joseph was exalted in Pharaoh's court, a number of things changed. He was given the privileges and trappings that accompanied his new office. These included a new name, an Egyptian one, Zaphenath-Paneah (Gen 41:45). We do not know what that name means, but we do know that the idea of renaming people was not uncommon in ancient times. Daniel and his friends were also given new names by King Nebuchadnezzar when he wanted them to serve in his court in Babylon (Dan 1:7). Such renaming was a sign of their assimilation into the dominant culture – in some ways it parallels the way many Africans were once given "Christian" names when they started school as a sign that they were going to orient themselves in terms of Western culture rather than their traditional African culture. The new name offered Joseph the opportunity to turn his back on his Hebrew identity. But he refused to do this. Although he would have used the Egyptian name in his official dealings, he did not deny who he was and acknowledged his relationship to his brothers.

As a further step towards assimilating Joseph into Egyptian culture, he was given an Egyptian wife, a woman named Asenath. Not only did she not know Joseph's God, but she was the daughter of a priest who served an Egyptian god. The description of her father as a "priest of On" means that he was associated with the worship in the city of On, which we know as Heliopolis. That city was a centre of sun worship. Asenath probably worshipped the sun god too, for her name can be interpreted as meaning "belonging to Neith", a sky goddess who was sometimes said to be the mother of Re or Ra, the sun god. Clearly Joseph found himself married to a woman who had strong roots in Egyptian religion.

For centuries people have been bothered by the idea that a godly man like Joseph was married to a woman who worshipped another god. Ancient Jewish interpreters tried to explain it away by arguing that Asenath was not really Egyptian. They claimed that she was actually the daughter of Shechem and Dinah, Joseph's sister (see Gen 34:1–4), who had been adopted by an Egyptian. This explanation involves quite a stretch of the imagination and is improbable; the more plausible and realistic interpretation is that Joseph married an Egyptian woman.

At that time, God had not yet given the law that forbade marriage with people who worshipped foreign gods – that command would come centuries later, in the law of Moses. So Joseph was not sinning when he married her. Nevertheless, he would have faced the same temptation that led to that law being given: the temptation to worship his wife's god. But we know from Joseph's subsequent actions that he did not succumb to that temptation.

It is interesting to note that as an Egyptian, Asenath was also an African. Thus Joseph's sons, the founders of the important tribes of Ephraim and Manasseh had African blood.

The most public of the perks that Joseph received was that he was issued with a chariot with men to run in front of it shouting "make way" whenever he rode out in it (Gen 41:43). In some respects, his situation was like that of government ministers who are issued with expensive cars and travel around our cities in motorcades preceded by police officers on motorbikes. Everyone else is expected to make way for them. Joseph was being given superstar treatment! What is problematic about this is that the Egyptian religion gave Pharaoh a godlike status. As Pharaoh's second-in-command, Joseph was elevated to somewhat similar status. After all, he had interpreted Pharaoh's dream, and Pharaoh had said, "Can we find anyone like this man, one in whom is the spirit of God?" (or "of the gods") (Gen 41:38). God is referred to in the singular in Genesis 41, probably because Joseph referred to him in the singular before Pharaoh, but Pharaoh probably understood the interpretation of the dream from his own religious outlook and did not ascribe it to the God of Israel but to the Egyptian gods.

Joseph's benefits seem to have been designed to integrate him into Egyptian culture and make him acceptable as a national leader. Joseph did not resist this treatment; he seems to have accepted it as something he would have to live with, whether or not he agreed with it. That is how leaders were treated in that culture.

Outwardly, Joseph now conformed to Egyptian culture. But his personal life shows that those closest to him, those who knew him personally, understood that he was a Hebrew man. His children were given Hebrew names. When his brothers came he made it clear to all that these men were his brothers. He eventually managed to get them settled in Goshen, separate from the Egyptians, because of their different culture. Joseph may have accepted some Egyptian ways, but though operating as an Egyptian, he never became an Egyptian at heart. His integrity remained; he was still a servant of the one true God, Creator of heaven and earth.

Integrity in stewardship

Whether in his boyhood home, in Potiphar's home, in prison, or in the palace, Joseph always rose to a position of trust. He was Jacob's trusted son; Potiphar noticed that all that Joseph did succeeded and he entrusted everything he had to him; the keeper of the prison put Joseph in charge of all the prisoners, and Pharaoh put Joseph in charge of the whole of Egypt. Only as regards the throne was Pharaoh greater than Joseph. Joseph was an excellent example of a steward-leader or manager.

To understand the concept of stewardship, it is important to understand three other words and how they are interrelated. These words are "power", "authority" and "accountability".

- *Power* is often defined as the "ability to translate intention into reality".
- *Authority* is the legitimate use of power (or the right to use power).
- *Accountability* is the process of explaining how power has been used.

The relationship between these words is well illustrated by the incident with Mrs Potiphar. Joseph had the power to sleep with her; he was a virile young man perfectly capable of having sexual relations with her, and she wanted him to use that power. But though he had the power to sleep with her, he had no authority to do so because she was not his wife. So he refused her advances, saying, "How then can I do this great wickedness and sin against God?" Joseph was aware that he was accountable to God for how he used his male potency.

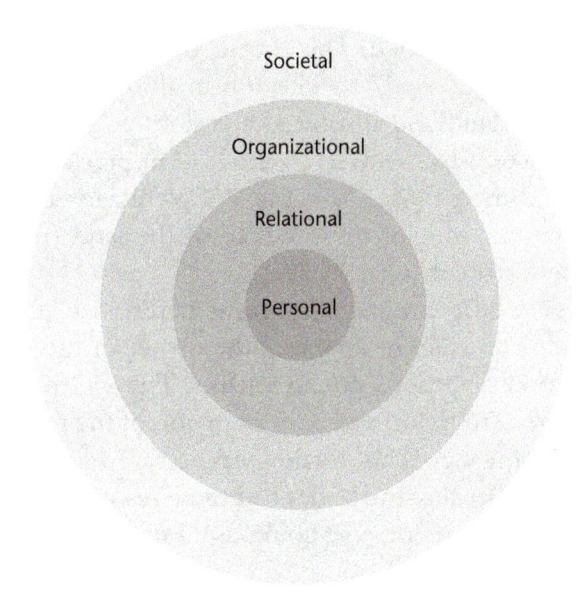

Figure 1. Model of Transformational Leadership[3]

Joseph's relationship with God affected his family and anyone who had dealings with him. Whatever organization he found himself in, be it his family, Potiphar's house, prison or the royal court, he permeated it with godly principles.

> Personal life transformation (that is, the development of character and wisdom in the individual life) of the leader, therefore, has to be the primary point of engagement for those who desire to change organizations, institutions and nations. As goes the leader so goes the institution. The heart of the leadership challenge is the heart of the leader.[4]

Eventually Joseph's good stewardship of power affected the whole of Egyptian society. He managed the seven good years so well that there were vast reservoirs of food to last through the seven bad years. It may be argued that Joseph enslaved the nations of Egypt and Canaan by making them give their money, livestock, land and eventually their

---

[3] From Dr Michael Wicker.
[4] Delanyo Adadevoh, *Personal Life Transformation in Biblical Perspective* (Orlando, FL.: International Leadership Foundation, 2013), 1, www.transformingleadership.com.

bodies to Pharaoh to get food. This is true, but it should be noted that after they became "enslaved" to Pharaoh in this way, Joseph allowed them back on the land and instituted a twenty percent tax on them. Their circumstances were no different from what prevailed in the seven years of plenty. During those seven years of plenty Joseph had advised Pharaoh to take one-fifth of the produce of the land (that is, twenty percent of it) and store it (Gen 41:34).

This is not very different from how some traditional African societies were organized. The chief or king was the owner of the land, and the people understood that they were his tenants. They cultivated and lived on the land allotted to them, and gave a portion of their produce to the king or traditional leader. This portion was reserved for a time of need in the community. Because the leader had these resources and was much wealthier than the community, he could use these resources to alleviate the suffering of his people.

The *Africa Bible Commentary* makes the following observations about Joseph:

> His objective was not to enslave the people but to make sure that the land of Egypt was managed well in the future … Though not stated, the idea was that some of each year's harvest would be kept in storage so that there would always be a good supply of food. The people could keep the remaining four-fifths.
>
> What we see here is an administrator with the people's interest at heart and an awareness of the need to provide for the future. He is the kind of leader that many African nations cry out for. The current generation should not be milked to the last drop by taxation and some of the income the government gets should be set aside for use by future generations.[5]

Joseph's stewardship strength became most apparent when he became the vizier (prime minister) of Egypt. Pharaoh made him second-in-command in Egypt, the most powerful man after Pharaoh. But Joseph did not let power go to his head. As chapter 41 of Genesis records, he

---

[5] Barnabe Assohoto and Samuel Ngewa, "Genesis", in *Africa Bible Commentary*, ed. Tokunboh Adeyemo (Grand Rapids: Zondervan; Nairobi, Kenya: WordAlive, 2006), 80.

immediately started working to put together the necessary resources to sustain the nation for the coming years of famine. He devoted many years to this task.

> And Joseph went out from Pharaoh's presence and travelled throughout Egypt. During the seven years of abundance the land produced plentifully. Joseph collected all the food produced in those seven years of abundance in Egypt and stored it in the cities. In each city he put the food grown in the fields surrounding it. Joseph stored up huge quantities of grain, like the sand of the sea; it was so much that he stopped keeping records because it was beyond measure. (Gen 41:46–49)

Pharaoh's dream had given him a vision of what was going to happen over the next fourteen years. Joseph provided an interpretation of the dream and recommended a strategy in light of the interpretation. Pharaoh entrusted him with managing the strategy's implementation. Management functions are crucial to make any vision successful.

It is worth noting that in the book of Genesis Joseph was always serving someone. He was always accountable not only to God but also to a human being. Those who are entrusted with anything must always give an account of how they have handled that trust.

By definition a steward is not an owner; a steward is a manager of something that belongs to someone else. The numerous parables on stewardship told by Jesus are instructive; I will touch on some of them later in the book. Joseph was entrusted with a key position in Egypt, and the sole reason for this trust was to ensure that Egypt would survive the seven years of famine. Joseph did a good job, so that by the time the famine started, Egypt was well prepared and all the nations around them came to Egypt for food.

It is sad when Africans have to go to other parts of the world for food. Few other regions are so abundantly blessed with fertile soil and good weather. Africans should be able to harvest so much that there would be more than enough food for Africa, and the rest of the world should be buying food from us. It is a mark of the lack of good stewardship, good planning, and good management that many go hungry.

In conclusion, Joseph's stewardship started with self-management, a consciousness that his body was not his own, it belonged to God.

Everywhere he went, he upheld his personal values. Because his personal values were informed by godly values, he was entrusted with responsibility. His personal integrity attracted people in authority, making them recognize that he was the one most suited to managing their resources. When given trust, he did not disappoint; he applied good management principles to ensure fruitfulness and success in all he did.

Joseph's Governance and Conflict Transformation

Angry, bitter and unforgiving people make terrible leaders. An angry person with a gun is someone to run away from. Joseph had all the power in Egypt, and when his brothers realized it, they were terrified. Surely he would be angry and vengeful, and surely he was going to use his power to destroy them. To their surprise and relief, he showed them love, mercy, gentleness, kindness and forgiveness. What a refreshing and startlingly good kind of leadership!

What made Joseph able to lead like this? His words to his brothers when they came to Egypt provide some hints about what had happened to him. First, when he revealed himself to them he said,

> I am your brother Joseph, the one you sold into Egypt! And now, do not be distressed and do not be angry with yourselves for selling me here, because it was to save lives that God sent me ahead of you … God sent me ahead of you to preserve for you a remnant on earth and to save your lives by a great deliverance. So then, it was not you who sent me here, but God. He made me father to Pharaoh, lord of his entire household and ruler of all Egypt. Now hurry back to my father and say to him, "This is what your son Joseph says: God has made me lord of all Egypt." (Gen 45:4–9)

When their father died, the brothers feared that perhaps Joseph had shown them kindness only because of his love for Jacob and his desire to bring him to Egypt. Now that Jacob was dead, the brothers feared that the dreaded retribution would come. But Joseph reassured them, saying

> Don't be afraid. Am I in the place of God? You intended to harm me, but God intended it for good to accomplish what is now being done, the saving of many lives. So then, don't be afraid. I will provide for you and your children. (Gen 50:19–21)

At some point, Joseph saw events from God's perspective, and he saw God working through everything that happened as part of his preparation to become what he now was. The New Testament scripture rings true, "And we know that in all things God works for the good of those who love him, who have been called according to his purpose" (Rom 8:28). God makes all things work together for good. Joseph was right that his brothers' intentions were evil. They had intended to harm him, even kill him, but God used that situation to send Joseph to Egypt.

The traumas that Joseph endured probably confused him. His language while he was in prison shows that he had not yet come to terms with what had happened to him – he was still crying out for justice and pleading with the cupbearer to bring his case to Pharaoh. At that point he was a wounded and perhaps bitter man. It seems he was able to settle the issues in his heart sometime after coming out of prison and seeing the sovereign hand of God behind all the events. He had been sold into slavery, but that led to his being in a key Egyptian leader's home, for Potiphar was captain of the guard, a high-ranking official. So high-ranking was Potiphar that Joseph was not put in an ordinary prison; he was sent to the prison where the king's prisoners were confined. Then there were the dreams of the baker and butler, and then Pharaoh's dreams and suddenly Joseph was elevated to number two in Egypt. God had indeed worked it all out for Joseph's good.

Did God make Joseph's brothers so wickedly disposed towards him? Probably not, but he did use their evil intentions against Joseph as a means to send Joseph to Egypt. Joseph saw his brothers as they really were in God's big scheme, mere men with clouded understanding of life. They had said "what will become of his dreams?" (Gen 37:20) not knowing that God was using even their schemes to accomplish his big agenda. Their minds were too small to see what God was doing; it was far beyond their imagination.

Joseph's ability to get above situations and see people from God's perspective was the secret to his ability to not retaliate. That was what helped him transform his relationship with his brothers from an ugly destructive conflict to an opportunity to show God's love. Joseph became a channel through which God could show himself to Jacob's family. As they encountered Joseph, they also encountered Joseph's God who was also their God. They saw a different way of leading through Joseph, and their experience with him brought out the best in them.

Modern conflict management training is designed to manage conflicts so that they do not escalate and become violent and destructive. We will be looking at this in more detail later in this book. But as Christians we should learn from Joseph that conflicts should not just be managed, they should be resolved or transformed. True victory in handling conflict comes from the ability to forgive and let go of an issue. Depending on how deeply a person has been hurt, forgiveness may not be easy. It may even be impossible to extend forgiveness without the help of supernatural power. But what we are seeking is not just conflict management but conflict transformation, the transforming of attitudes and behaviours.

For conflicts to be transformed, they need to be seen differently. Negative perceptions need to be overcome and reassuring, constructive behaviours need to replace hostility. Such an environment makes for constructive leadership; unmanaged conflicts create ungovernable environments.

Joseph was able to defuse the conflict in his home and create an environment that was conducive for God to accomplish his purposes through his family. Families, institutions and countries that have learned to move from destructive to constructive conflicts will move forward positively.

The best way to transform conflicts, as we learn from Joseph's story, is for one's inner conflict with God to be settled. Only when peace with God is found can a person live at peace with others. Joseph could have been a very destructive loose cannon if his inner conflicts had not been resolved. As it worked out, the peace in Joseph's heart transformed the volatile situation with his brothers into a sweet and pleasant one. Instead of an explosive volcano, the brothers encountered still waters in Joseph. Conflicts are transformed through transformed individuals.

Before we go on to deal with the relevance of Joseph's experience to our contemporary African situation and the practical applications today, let us look at someone who is the antithesis of Joseph – the prophet Jonah. He is an example of how not to use power and how not to represent God.

For Discussion

1. How does Joseph's story feed into the bigger story in terms of God's creation of the nation of Israel and his desire to make them into his own people?
2. Why do you think God put Joseph through all the trouble he experienced?
3. How did Joseph use his God-given power for the benefit of Egypt, Israel and the surrounding nations?
4. Compare Joseph's use of power with
    a) his brothers' use of power,
    b) Mrs Potiphar's use of power, and
    c) Pharaoh's use of power.

4

JONAH'S FAILURE AS A STEWARD

We encounter the prophet Jonah in two places in Scripture, once in 2 Kings 14:24 and again in the book of Jonah. It is a short book, and I recommend that you reread it before reading the rest of this chapter.

A Wild Horse

Many believers today find themselves in privileged positions. God has given them jobs they never thought they would have, cars they never thought they would drive, and houses they never dreamed they would live in. But they do not seek to use these blessings for the good of others. Instead, the blessings are seen as ends in themselves and their owners think they have arrived and are entitled to relax and enjoy themselves. They fail to appreciate the bigger purpose of God in blessing them so much.

In some respects the prophet Jonah was like these people. His story illustrates how someone who knows God's blessings can still be at cross-purposes with him and can bolt like a wild horse when God calls on him or her to do something. God works in partnership with us and only when our hearts are aligned with God's heart can we be of optimal use. When we are like Jonah and our hearts are not in accord with God's heart, we misrepresent God and can even hinder what he is trying to do.

Unlike Joseph who learned to overcome personal hurts and the pain of injustice and so forgave and reconciled with his brothers, Jonah was bitter and angry with God for not doing what he wanted. Jonah was also an intolerant and unforgiving nationalist. When God told him to go to Nineveh, and warn the Assyrians of impending judgement because of their wickedness, it was too much for Jonah to take. He hated the Assyrians so much that all he wanted was to see them destroyed. He fought with God because he felt that God was too gracious and compassionate towards them:

> He prayed to the LORD, "Isn't this what I said, LORD, when I was still at home? That is what I tried to forestall by fleeing to Tarshish. I knew that you are a gracious and compassionate God, slow to anger and abounding in love, a God who relents from sending calamity." (Jonah 4:2)

Jonah and the Assyrians

The Assyrians were a superpower in Jonah's time. The annals of the Assyrian king Shalmanesser III (858–824 BC) record that Israel had paid them tribute since the days of King Jehu, who reigned from about 841–813 BC. This relationship continued in the days of Jonah, when Jeroboam II (782–753) ruled over Israel (2 Kgs 14:25). Israel was thus Assyria's vassal, enjoying goodwill as long as it paid tribute.

The Assyrians maintained their power by unleashing unprecedented cruelty on any who opposed them. They gloried in their torture techniques and invented many ways to inflict pain on their enemies, boasting of how they made conquered nations suffer. They piled up mounds of human heads, they skinned people alive and hung their skin on city walls, they impaled people on sharp poles and left them hanging there to die. Boastful inscriptions on the walls of Assyrian palaces celebrated their cruelty and savagery. Each king sought to prove himself more heinous than the one who preceded him. Here is an account dating from the time of Shalmanesser III's predecessor, Ashurnasirpal II (883–858 BC):

> I flayed as many nobles as had rebelled against me and draped their skins over the pile; some I spread out within the pile, some I erected on stakes upon the pile, (and) some I placed on stakes around about the pile. I flayed many right through my land (and) draped their skins over the walls. I slashed the flesh of the eunuchs and of the royal eunuchs who were guilty.[1]

And here is another account:

> I felled 50 of their fighting men with the sword, burnt 200 captives from them, and defeated in a battle on the plain 332 troops ... With their blood I dyed the mountain red like red wool, and the rest of them the ravines and torrents of the mountain swallowed. I carried off captives and possessions from them. I cut off the heads of their fighters and built with them a tower before their city. I burnt their adolescent boys and girls.[2]

These were the kind of people Jonah would be interacting with in Nineveh. Nor are these the only passages I could have quoted, for archaeologists have found enough material from Assyrian sources to fill a two-volume work with a total of over eight hundred pages, called *Ancient Records of Assyria and Babylonia*.[3]

The Assyrians were not only cruel, they were also extremely proud. To illustrate this, I will quote some words from the last king of Assyria, even though they date from after Jonah's time.

> I am Assurbanipal, the great [king], the mighty king, king of the universe, king of Assyria, king of the [four regions (of the world)]; offspring of the loins of Esarhaddon, king of the universe, king of Assyria, viceroy of Babylon, king of Sumer and Akkad; grandson of Sennacherib, king of the universe, king of Assyria. The great gods in their council (gathering) decreed (for me) a favorable destiny, and granted (me) a receptive mind

---

[1] Mehmet-Ali Ataç, *The Mythology of Kingship in Neo-Assyrian Art* (Cambridge: Cambridge University Press, 2010), 40.
[2] John Robertson, *Iraq: A History* (London: Oneworld Publications, 2015).
[3] Daniel David Luckenbill (Vol 2), *Ancient Records of Assyria and Babylon* (Chicago: University of Chicago Press, 1927).

(lit., wide ear). They caused me *(lit.,* my belly) to grasp all of the scribal art. In the assembly of princes, they magnified my name, they made my rule powerful. Might, virility, enormous power, they granted me.

When God commanded Jonah to go to Nineveh and prophesy to them, Jonah disagreed with God's instruction so passionately that he set out to get as far away from Nineveh as he could. He boarded a ship bound for Tarshish, which lay more than 3000 kilometres (2000 miles) to the west in what is now Spain. By contrast the distance by land to Nineveh from Israel was a mere 800 km (500 miles). Jonah did not care that the journey by sea was far longer than the land journey God had commanded. He knew when he boarded the boat that under normal circumstances it would take months before he could get back to Joppa.

Jonah knew that God operates in partnership with his prophets, and Jonah was making it quite clear that he was not interested in proclaiming anything about God's grace and compassion to the Assyrians. As far as Jonah was concerned, they were not people to be talked to. All they deserved was death.

Jonah's behaviour shows that he failed to understand three aspects of God's dealings with humanity:

- God blesses some so that through them others will be blessed.
- Selfish or national interests should not come before God's interests.
- God's spokesperson must see as God sees and feel as God feels.

God blesses to bless others

As we saw when looking at Joseph's family, God had told Abram:

> I will make you into a great nation, and I will bless you; I will make your name great, and you will be a blessing. I will bless those who bless you, and whoever curses you I will curse; and all peoples on earth will be blessed through you. (Gen 12:1–3)

The rest of the book of Genesis and the Old Testament tell us that this nation was the one that came to be known as Israel. Israel's divine mandate was to be a blessing to the nations. As other nations looked at

Israel they were to see how good is the God of Israel, the one true God, and turn to him.

In Jonah's day, Israel had not been faithful to God. They were threatened with removal from the land because of their sin. They had forgotten that the reason for their existence was to represent God to the rest of the world and be the channel through which he could reach the world and bless it. Jonah too ignored this part of God's plan. He would not accept that God's instruction to go to Nineveh was part of God's grand design to reach the world through Israel. Jonah was not even willing to take another nation a message from God.

Israel as a nation had first-hand experience of God's mighty power. God had revealed himself to them, and given them his laws. His prophets had an intimate knowledge of God; he would especially reveal himself to them and they knew his heart. They should have been transformed into his image, so that seeing them should have been like seeing God. They were called to represent God in their words, their attitudes and their actions. Jonah's assignment to go to Nineveh would thus have given the Assyrians an opportunity to be exposed to the one true God who was also the God of Israel.

The same applies to us today, as Peter makes clear when he describes the role of believers and of the church:

> But you are a chosen race, a royal priesthood, a holy nation, a people for his own possession, that you may proclaim the excellencies of him who called you out of darkness into his marvellous light. Once you were not a people, but now you are God's people; once you had not received mercy, but now you have received mercy. (1 Pet 2:9–10)

Just as Israel represented God to the nations in the Old Testament, so the church is a nation within a nation and is called to proclaim him to the rest of the world. When we receive blessings, they are not an end in themselves; God's blessings are meant to be used to further his gospel.

Selfish or national interests should not come before God's interests

Jonah saw himself first as an Israelite and only secondarily as a servant of God. He put his own interests and the interests of his people and his nation ahead of the interests of God. He liked to give prophecies that were favourable to Israel such as the one recorded in 2 Kings 14:25 – that sort of message aligned with his strong patriotism. But when it came to dealing with the people of Nineveh, he acted more like a patriotic Israelite than a prophet of God.

Clearly Jonah was still a work in progress. God has to work in us his servants so that we learn not to let our personal interests stand in the way of God's interests. Jonah was not there yet. He was like an unbroken horse, kicking and bucking and trying to get God off his back. He was the complete opposite of Joseph who had become like an obedient horse, with its strength harnessed and subject to the master's desires.

Jesus used a different metaphor to make the same point when he said that those who follow him must deny themselves and take up their cross (Luke 9:23). In other words, those who want to serve God need to die to self. In Jonah's case, dying to self meant that he would have to abandon three things:

1) *The desire for self-preservation.* Serving God calls for sacrifice. Jonah must have been aware that he would face personal danger if he went into enemy territory and proclaimed a message from his and Israel's God. It was quite possible that he would die if he obeyed God. Many other biblical characters did die in the process of obeying God's instructions, as the writer of the letter to the Hebrews points out (Heb 11:24–26). But God does not judge success by the standards of the world, and many of those who died left a powerful legacy. Jonah had to learn to trust God no matter what happened.

2) *His own people and culture.* Jonah's fellow Israelites would not have thought him patriotic if he helped Nineveh escape judgement. Jonah had to learn to be God's spokesman rather than a national spokesman. He had to confront himself and his own culture with God's word, God's way, the kingdom way. We fall into the same trap as Jonah when we value our own people and culture above godly living. For instance, some will not vote a Christian with godly values into office simply because that person is from a different tribe. We ignore all their virtues and focus only on the womb that bore them.

3) *The idea that he could run away from God's call.* Jonah tried it and found out the hard way that you cannot run from God (Rom 11:29). God's supernatural interventions that thwarted Jonah's voyage to Tarshish illustrate the extent to which God will go to get his servant to fulfil his mission and do what God wants. When God calls, there is no point in rebellion or backsliding, the call will not allow us rest until it is accomplished.

Both Jonah and Joseph had to die to self before God could use them. God's processes with them were different, but the principle is the same. Their personal and national interests had to become subservient to God's interests.

God's spokesperson must see as he sees and feel as he feels

Jonah's problem was that his emotions were different from God's emotions. When he was back on land after his time in the belly of the fish, and was again commanded to go to Nineveh, he was compliant. He realized that God was very serious about this issue, and though he still felt disgusted by the Assyrians, he went. He obeyed and delivered the message, but he failed to see what God was seeing as the people of Nineveh cried out to God, fasting and praying. Indeed, he fiercely disagreed with God's merciful response to their repentance.

So God used an object lesson to help Jonah see things from his perspective. He allowed a vine to grow and shade Jonah from the fierce heat of the sun, and then he allowed the vine to wither. Jonah was furious when it died – it was the last straw, after his other disappointment when God relented and did not destroy Nineveh. Jonah's reaction clearly shows that he was more concerned about the vine that gave him comfort than about pleasing the God who provided the vine. He was more preoccupied with the blessings God gave than with the God who blessed.

So God pointed out that the things that angered Jonah were minor issues to God, and the things that God considered important were minor to Jonah,

> But the LORD said, "You have been concerned about this plant, though you did not tend it or make it grow. It sprang up overnight and died overnight. And should I not have concern

for the great city of Nineveh, in which there are more than a hundred and twenty thousand people who cannot tell their right hand from their left – and also many animals?" (Jonah 4:10–11)

These are the closing words of the book of Jonah. Right up to the last sentence in the book, Jonah was in conflict with God. He did not feel as God felt, he fiercely disagreed with God right to the end. The fact that we do have the book of Jonah, especially if he wrote it himself, may be testimony to his eventual change of heart, but it is not recorded in the Bible.

Not only was God concerned about the people of Nineveh, he was also concerned about their animals. Livestock were a measure of the wealth of a people in ancient times, just as they were until recently in some parts of Africa, and so the reference to animals in this verse can be interpreted as evidence of God's concern not just for the people of Nineveh but also for their economic well-being. To assume that God only cares about the spiritual well-being of a people and not their material well-being is to dichotomize the sacred and the secular. That is Greek thinking, not biblical thinking. God wants to bless people both spiritually and materially.

Discipleship and Nation Building

God's call to his church is to go and make disciples of all nations. That is the mission. That must be the main activity of all Christians. Whatever we do, wherever we are, we must ask how we are contributing to making disciples of all nations. Leading people to a saving knowledge of Christ and then helping them to become obedient or mature believers through teaching and modelling true Christianity is the discipleship process.

The way that God has chosen to win the world back to himself is through having people model the kind of life he wants for all, in both word and deed. People like Joseph and Jonah in the Old Testament illustrate how God worked through individuals but ultimately through the nation of Israel to be a light for the nations. In God's ideal plan, ancient Israel would have been a bright shining light in the darkness and confusion of the world.

In the New Testament, God works through Christ-like individuals and through his church, both local and universal. He wants us to be a bright light to the world, and he wants this light to illuminate not only individuals but also families, communities, ethnicities and nations. As Christ said:

> You are the light of the world. A town built on a hill cannot be hidden. Neither do people light a lamp and put it under a bowl. Instead they put it on its stand, and it gives light to everyone in the house. In the same way, let your light shine before others, that they may see your good deeds and glorify your Father in heaven. (Matt 5:14–16)

African Christians and nations which are now statistically predominantly Christian need to start putting that scripture into practice. So in the next section of the book we will explore how the African church can engage and influence contemporary African leadership practice. We will consider some of the parallels between our experience in Africa today and the experience of men like Joseph and Jonah. My prayer is that your engagement with our world will not be like Jonah's but will be as effective and godly as was Joseph's with the pagan Egyptian world in which he found himself.

For Discussion

1. Compare Joseph's attitude with Jonah's.
2. Do you know people who are more like Jonah or more like Joseph?
3. What about you? Which of these men do you resemble?
4. The reference to cattle in Jonah 4:11 shows God's concern for Nineveh's wealth and material well-being. Should the church be concerned with the economic performance of nations? If so how can it be involved in running nations?

5

FORGIVENESS AND RECONCILIATION

The stories of Joseph and Jonah resonate with us because many of us can identify with their emotional experiences. We know what it is to feel bitterness and anger in the face of injustice. We too have been entrusted with resources that we need to use well. And so we can learn from the way they responded to their circumstances and can apply what we learn in an African context.

Africa's Pain

In chapter 3, we saw how Joseph was raised in a broken polygamous family, filled with rivalry between the adults and conflict among the adult children. We saw how this led to violence that destroyed the familiar routines of his life and all his hopes for the future. And although this violence began in the family, it spilled over and involved people from other nations who were slave traders, and the world powers of the day. Does that sound at all familiar to you?

This type of pain is not restricted to individuals in families. It affects whole societies in the form of tribal rivalries. The fact that Africans were already divided made colonization easier. And the policies of the colonizers helped to entrench ethnic divisions by favouring some groups over others and by partitioning countries without regard for the existing ethnic boundaries. The Rwandan genocide of 1994 is among the most famous examples of the fruit such rivalry can produce. Neighbour killed neighbour purely because the one was Hutu and the other Tutsi. Almost one million people died in a hundred days of terrible genocide.

In Zimbabwe, tribal divisions between the Shona and Ndebele can be traced back almost two hundred years. Although these divisions are nowhere near as deep as those found elsewhere in Africa, there have still been instances of state-sponsored violence directed against one tribe. (The Gukurahundi massacres were well documented by the Catholic Commission for Justice and Peace.)

Similar stories are found throughout Africa. Simmering tribal tensions brew underneath the veneer of calm and peace in even those countries that are viewed as peaceful. We should never forget that Rwanda was regarded as ninety percent Christian at the time of the genocide, yet tribe rose against tribe and even some Christian bishops fanned tribal divisions from their pulpits.

Do you see the similarity with the rivalries within the patriarchal family into which Joseph was born? They were the first of God's chosen people, but they too sinned and failed to live in peace and harmony.

Sometimes these tribal divisions are exacerbated by religious divisions. I was in Nairobi, Kenya, on 21 September 2013 when Al Shabaab militants took over the Westgate Mall. I had in fact been in that mall the previous day. Not surprisingly, the events that followed are deeply embedded in my memory. The senseless killing of innocent civilians was unbelievable, yet it was happening right before me, in a place I knew.

The Al Shabaab militants are religious (Islamic) extremists. Such extremism is not unique to Kenya; Boko Haram is causing similar mayhem in Nigeria – their abduction of more than two hundred girls in Nigeria in April 2014 enraged the world. In other North African countries there has long been much hostility to Christianity, to the point of killing Christians.

Much of the conflict in Joseph's family came about because Jacob provided poor leadership – and that too is a source of Africa's pain. Colonialism gave Africa a legacy of exploitative and oppressive leadership.[1] Africans were subjugated, and Africa's natural resources were exploited for the benefit of other nations. Africa was governed in a

---

[1] For an extreme example of colonial policy towards Africa, see Adam Hochschild, *King Leopold's Ghost: A Story of Greed, Terror, and Heroism in Colonial Africa* (Boston: Houghton Mifflin, 1999).

way that would never have been tolerated in the colonizers' countries of origin, and the colonizers lived in a style they could never have enjoyed in the lands from which they came. They built themselves homes that were three and four times the size of the homes they had been raised in and gave themselves vast tracts of land. They maintained power through heavy-handed police forces that operated in ways they would never do back home. They destroyed much of Africa's traditional leadership and replaced it with their own style of leadership.

For many Africans, colonial leadership became the model for leadership – and we have perfected that style. Our police are generally hostile to the population and often use brutal force unnecessarily. Police roadblocks are commonplace, whereas in other countries they are used only when there is a heightened threat of attack. Our roadblocks are often places of extortion, where police find ridiculous reasons to force people into paying them money as bribes.

I have seen the abuses of the Zimbabwean citizenry by the police, especially between 2000 and 2008. The police are now more restrained. Because I have served as a church leader in various capacities (pastor, administrator and educator), I have heard first-hand testimonies of atrocities that took place during that time of state-sponsored anarchy. Teachers were targeted in rural Zimbabwe, accused of mobilizing the people against the ruling party. The police allowed party thugs to rape and pillage at will. Teachers told me horrifying stories of having to watch their spouses raped. One man told me that when the police came to quell food riots in his area, they forced him to open his gate and then beat him, his wife and his children with their batons. He had never felt so useless and impotent as a man as he did that day.

Such painful episodes can easily become a root of bitterness. The mere memory of an event like that is emotionally draining and can be the justifiable seed of a quest for revenge. Joseph must have known similar emotions as he remembered what his brothers and Potiphar's wife had done to him. Jonah, too, knew of the cruelty and injustice of Assyria, the superpower in his day. But unlike Joseph, who could forgive those who caused his pain, Jonah allowed the pain to infect his heart and became stubborn, xenophobic, angry, unforgiving and bitter.

Joseph must also have experienced a sense of abandonment when the cupbearer, who had promised to work for his release, did nothing to fulfil that promise once he was reinstated as Joseph had predicted. We too know the pain of unmet expectations. The promises and high hopes that came with independence were soon dashed by the realization that the new leaders were not the saviours we had hoped for. We had merely exchanged one set of oppressors and exploiters for another. Was it for this that we had supported liberation movements dedicated to overthrowing oppressive white regimes and redressing the imbalances that came with colonialism? Was it for this that many died in wars against colonial powers and others endured unimaginable hardship? Many lost children; others bear deep physical and emotional scars. Some cannot even speak of the pain they endured – and on that is heaped the pain that their leaders have betrayed the noble goals for which they fought.

While we no longer share Joseph's experience of physical slavery, we do share his experience of economic exploitation. We used to celebrate when international bodies granted our countries huge loans. But we were kept in the dark about the terms on which these loans were given and the amounts that would have to be paid in interest. Western countries have reaped great financial harvests from the interest accrued. Today we ask whether such loans were really an attempt to help or merely another example of exploitation of poor countries by rich countries.

It may be argued that these loans were given to accomplish specific objectives like building or refurbishing power stations, fixing roads and railway networks, or meeting water-related needs by building dams, providing clean water and the like. If the funds had been used for the designated purposes, the income generated could have repaid the loans. However, the sad truth is that we know very little about how these funds were used. Dambisa Moyo[2] and scholars such as Ndikumana and Boyce[3] claim that much of the money was privatized. Vast sums intended for Africa never reached Africa; instead, the money was diverted into private accounts, often in the very same banks that issued the loan. So we in Africa see no sign of the promised roads, electricity, clean water or functional railway systems for which the loan was taken, but we still

---

[2] Moyo, *Dead Aid*.
[3] Leonce Ndikumana and James Boyce, *Africa's Odious Debts: How Foreign Loans and Capital Flight Bled a Continent* (London: Zed Books, 2011).

have to repay a loan that most likely funded houses, cars, businesses, girlfriends' houses and pocket money for someone in power.

In a desperate search for solutions to their pain, the poor turn to the church. But there they often find only more pain. They are constantly asked to use what little money they have as a "seed" in the hope of harvesting a miracle that will deliver them from their problems. Their breakthrough is always said to be "coming", but it never arrives. Sometimes they have to walk home after a church meeting, having left everything they have at the altar. Meanwhile the so-called "man of God" drives back to his mansion in one of his fleet of luxury cars – if he did not fly to the meeting in his private jet or helicopter. He wears designer clothes and expensive perfume as he again and again promises the poor a breakthrough if they pay their dues.

Who will see the plight of the poor? Who will truly make their lives better? From broken polygamous families to dysfunctional countries, the African situation cries out for sound and constructive leadership. Africa waits with reddened eyes and great anticipation for the emergence of true, godly African statesmen and women, who will genuinely care and provide good leadership.

Africa's Comfort

Africa's pain is real and most Africans live with it in one form or another. However, that is not the whole story. To focus on the one without mentioning the other would be like telling the story of Joseph and focusing only on his enslavement and pain, with all their potential to rouse bitterness and anger. But we know that Joseph also experienced blessings and was comforted. We see this even in the name he gave his firstborn son, Manasseh, which literally means "forgetful". We in Africa have also experienced blessings that must not be ignored.

Material comfort
Over the past fifty years the quality of life of many Africans has improved. Whereas once there were few vehicles of any kind in Africa, today the streets of African cities are clogged with cars, many of them luxury vehicles. It has been said that there are more Mercedes-Benz vehicles

in Nigeria than there are in Germany where they are made. Colonial houses now look like cottages compared to the houses some Africans have built. I have seen these mansions in Zimbabwe, Botswana, South Africa, Ghana, Nigeria, Burundi and Kenya. They would not be out of place in any Western city – except for the poverty and squalor that surround them.

The past fifty years have also seen a dramatic shift as many Africans have moved from rural areas to urban and even international centres. Some have moved from the depths of rural poverty to places where they enjoy a privileged lifestyle and the highest quality of life. And although some have acquired these blessings by dishonest means, that is certainly not true of all. There are many who have used their entrepreneurial skills to create wealth for themselves and provide employment for others. Some have gone to university and become business executives, others have joined the ranks of doctors and lawyers and other professionals, and still others have entered the public service where they have risen to high-ranking positions. Their lives may not have been easy, but today they have great power and affluence and can affect the course of events in their institutions and societies.

Of particular interest is the number of professing Christians in key leadership positions on the continent. If all these people lived godly lives and governed in a godly manner the continent would be transformed overnight. Sadly, many professing Christians, though now comforted, do not act like Joseph and do as much as they could or should to help transform their societies.

Let me reiterate, I am not suggesting that none of these people live godly lives. There are many who do, and many of them experience the blessing of the orderly life that is the result of daily applying godly principles. Their integrity and diligence have brought them promotions and won them favour, and like Joseph, they have seen that God has exalted them to a place of power and wealth beyond their wildest dreams.

Perhaps what those who enjoy these blessings now need is a vision to understand why God has raised them to such positions. Is God's blessing intended purely to promote their personal comfort, or does God want to do something more?

Spiritual comfort

So far, I have been speaking only of material blessings. But Joseph's comfort was also rooted in his spiritual life and his trust in God. So we should not neglect the spiritual comfort we too have been given. Missionaries were one channel through which spiritual comfort came to this continent, and we should thank God for them.

In saying this, I am not denying the element of truth in the words sometimes attributed to Jomo Kenyatta: "When the missionaries arrived, the Africans had the land and the missionaries had the Bible. They taught how to pray with our eyes closed. When we opened them, they had the land and we had the Bible." It is easy to find online information about King Leopold's instructions to missionaries telling them to promote Belgian interests in the Congo. Many missionaries did indeed come with a mandate from their colonial governments, and this political agenda influenced some of what they did. The missionaries were not sinless saints! (But then, neither was Joseph, as we saw when we talked about his pride, nor Jonah, who hated the people of Nineveh.)

But for all the failings of missionaries, we would be dishonest to ignore the fact that some missionaries did put their allegiance to God above their allegiance to their country and bravely stood for African causes. Think of David Livingstone, whose statue still stands at the Victoria Falls. Though we know that the Tonga people who first showed Livingstone the falls called them Mosi-oa-Tunya ("The Smoke that Thunders"), the name he gave them is still honoured today. Why is this? A trip to Zimbabwe's national archives will reveal what Livingstone did for the people of Zimbabwe, Zambia and Malawi. Livingstone, unlike many, had the courage to speak for Africans. He wrote to the British queen, advising her that if what was being done to Africans by Europeans were done in Scotland, every Scotsman who calls himself a man would rise up and fight for his land. Livingstone was honoured and loved by our fathers; we dare not dishonour him. He saw Africa through African eyes.

Many successful Africans (including President Mugabe of Zimbabwe) have to admit that, like it or not, missionaries played some role in their education. They built schools in the rural areas and made education accessible. They provided hospitals, and even today their infrastructural investments still stand as a testimony to their positive contribution to African society.

The education missionaries brought to Africa was rooted in the Bible and motivated by a godly desire to love and serve. However, the missionaries were children of their culture and upbringing, and sometimes their cultural understandings and stereotyping influenced their attitudes and led them to buy into the agendas of the colonial educational system. In those areas that were part of the British Empire, education was primarily designed to help extend that empire. Thus the template for the entire school system was based on examples developed in the West and for the West. As such, it privileged English as the medium of instruction, ensuring that people who were literate in colonial languages were at an advantage when seeking employment. It also provided basic skills in mathematics and literacy that were intended to enable educated Africans to participate in colonial economic and administrative systems.

The missionary education system also contributed to the spread of Christianity as a global religion, infusing mission-educated Africans with Judeo-Christian values. This type of cultural domination is not new. British missionary schools were following the same model the Babylonians used when they tried to change Daniel and his friends through changing their names, diet, language and religion (Dan 1:3–7). The Babylonians did not manage to wipe out the Jewish religion, but their cultural domination resulted in many Jewish people in Jesus' day having Aramaic (the language of Babylon) as their first language. Similarly, Greek cultural domination following the conquests of Alexander the Great explains why the New Testament was written in Greek. And Greek thinking still shapes the way we think about democratic government.

The colonial education system achieved its goal to the extent that English has now become a national language in many former British colonies (French has a similar status in former French colonies). But at the same time, the colonial education system laid the groundwork for its own defeat, for it created a class of individuals within Africa who developed the tools to articulate, in the colonizers' own language, a dialogue of resistance to colonial oppression.

The rise of African nationalism was one unanticipated consequence of colonial education and can largely be attributed to the contribution of missionaries. They understood that all were created equal before God, and so truly God-sent missionaries, motivated by love, were inevitably on a collision path with their colonial colleagues who sought to plunder and subjugate. For example, the colonial system would not educate Africans to university level, but the missionaries insisted on doing so.

The first Southern African university with colonial roots to admit black people was the University of Fort Hare in South Africa, a missionary initiative. It was where Zimbabwean president Robert Mugabe studied. So did other prominent Zimbabwean political leaders, including Joshua Nkomo and Herbert Chitepo. Prominent South African alumni include former South African president Nelson Mandela, Govan Mbeki (former president Thabo Mbeki's father), Oliver Tambo, Archbishop Desmond Tutu and Mangosuthu Buthelezi. This university was also the alma mater of Sir Seretse Khama of Botswana, Julius Nyerere of Tanzania and Kenneth Kaunda of Zambia.

The missionary legacy is thus mixed. Like all human beings, the missionaries had their failings, but a fair assessment of their contribution in Africa has to say they have been a blessing and a source of comfort to a suffering people. Much good has come from their work. We would not be wrong to paraphrase the words of Joseph, and say that "God sent them here for good".

Africa's Kindness

Joseph came to realize that it was God who had sent him to Egypt ahead of his brothers. Once he understood that, he could rise above the conflict in his home. He saw his brothers from God's perspective and he understood what God was doing. He therefore had the bigger picture. If we are to engage with our world, we too must learn to see as God sees, we must regard one another according to the Spirit and not the flesh, and must live out the Christian values we claim to hold dear. Doing so will involve showing kindness and forgiveness in our relations with other races and ethnicities, in our economic lives, and in relation to our fellow Africans who follow other religions.

Transcending racial barriers

One of the closest contemporary parallels to the story of Joseph is the story of Nelson Mandela. He suffered greatly, and yet when he walked out of prison, he extended forgiveness to the white apartheid society that had imprisoned him for twenty-seven years. He became the most celebrated African political leader in our generation. Much of the peace and progress South Africa has experienced to date flows from his legacy of forgiveness. Somehow when he came out of prison, he was a man with a heart big enough to rise above demanding retribution for the pain and injustice that he had suffered and to extend a hand of reconciliation to the white people who caused it. Mandela may or may not have been a Christian, and there are those who question some of the policies he adopted, but the influence of Christianity on his values and thinking is unquestionable.

But while Nelson Mandela proved to be a leader who not only suffered like Joseph but also forgave like Joseph and led like Joseph, there are few who follow in his footsteps. Africans in general have not yet gone past the pain of colonialism. This is illustrated by the concern expressed at the fact that Ian Khama, the current president of Botswana, has a white mother. There was even deeper shock when the unexpected death of President Michael Sata of Zambia resulted in his vice-president, a white Zambian by the name of Guy Scott, becoming acting president of Zambia. How could a white person be leading an African country! Sentiments like "this is giving Africa back to the whites" were expressed. Clearly President Sata had been able to see past Guy Scott's skin colour and focus on his character. If only others could do the same!

I once submitted an article to a Zimbabwean newspaper in which I suggested that white people are Zimbabweans too and that we ought to move past historic leadership failures and build a future for our nation based on leaders who merit appointment to the trust of representing us all. Here is some of what I wrote:

> When I, as a black Zimbabwean think of the way we treat white people who were born in this country I feel saddened and embarrassed. Yes their ancestors oppressed us, and all the rest of the rhetoric, but that does not justify the way they are treated today. Whites are ostracized and treated as second-class citizens; they are not seen as full Zimbabweans, and just

because they were born white they are very unlikely to have certain opportunities available to blacks.

Several white people could make very good presidents for Zimbabwe if allowed and enabled to aspire to do that. At the most difficult time in the history of white Zimbabweans, some have proudly represented the country in arenas like world sporting events and refused to give up their citizenship. They could have been bitter and resentful, but something in their character is outstanding and rises above the circumstances. They are bigger than their own people's hatred of blacks, bigger than black people's hatred of whites; showing the world that Zimbabweans could be good, loving and forgiving people. People can feel safe around us when they see kindness, love and even joyfulness. Angry and hateful people are scary; people want to run away from them, they do not feel safe around them. Never mind what made them angry and hateful, it is just not safe to be around angry and hateful people.

A further reason that I think some whites could make a good president is that their conduct is exemplary, often not only embracing biblical values but true Zimbabwean values that we are proud of. In a world where promiscuity is the norm and young girls just give themselves away to young men, some young white women do it the proper way, upholding some deep African values by insisting that as Zimbabweans they will get married in the Zimbabwean way. Young men come with a bride price to the girl's family and gave dignity and honour to the family by not taking their daughter without being given her hand in marriage. You don't just come and take a Zimbabwean girl and make her your wife. No! You must pay a bride price; the family must give her to you. There are some good things in African culture, and this is one of them.[4]

In 1963 Martin Luther King's speech "I Have a Dream!" outlined some very important principles for race relations. He stressed the importance of judging people by merit rather than by race:

---

[4] The article was never published.

> I have a dream that one day this nation will rise up and live out the true meaning of its creed: "We hold these truths to be self-evident: that all men are created equal."
>
> I have a dream that one day on the red hills of Georgia the sons of former slaves and the sons of former slave owners will be able to sit down together at the table of brotherhood... .
>
> I have a dream that my four little children will one day live in a nation where they will not be judged by the colour of their skin but by the content of their character.[5]

The quality of character shown by Martin Luther King's generation broke the back of racism in America. Racism capitulated in the face of non-violent resistance that appealed to the highest human virtues. The African Americans protested in an honourable manner that shamed hate-filled persons for their prejudice and racism. Their actions made it possible for Barack Obama, an African American of Kenyan descent, to serve as the 44th President of the United States – something that would have been unthinkable in 1963.

I too have a dream. It is that one day Zimbabwe will accept people of African, European, Indian, Chinese and any other racial descent as full Zimbabweans with full citizenship rights. Nobody chooses their country of birth or the colour of their skin; it is therefore inhuman and cruel to mistreat people and prejudge them on that basis. People should be judged on the quality of their character and abilities, not on the failures or feuds of past generations. We must stop thinking in terms that bring Kung-Fu films to mind: "A hundred years ago your great-uncle killed my grandfather ..." and the blows start flying. We must rise above such nonsensical thinking.

If Africa is going to move forward in the next generation, we need to move past the politics of colour and let the best people we have represent us in the best way they can. Zambia made a bold statement by having a white vice-president who successfully transitioned power to the next elected president. Africa needs to follow this example. *Chokwadi takadya nhokodzezvironda* ("We suffered so much and had nothing to eat, and in our desperation we ate the scabs of our wounds"). Let us

---
[5] "Special Collections, March on Washington, Part 17". Open Vault at WGBH. August 28, 1963.

move on from sitting and eating the scabs from our wounds. That only reopens them. It is time to heal. We need to be more like Joseph than like Jonah.

Transcending tribal barriers

Think what would have happened if Joseph had not reconciled with his brothers. Would we have seen centuries of hatred and conflict between Ephraim and Manasseh (the two tribes that arose from his descendants) and the tribes fathered by Jacob's other sons? By choosing to be reconciled rather than to seek revenge, Joseph brought an end to decades of bitter conflict that had started with the dysfunctional relationship between Jacob and his four wives (or, more accurately, his two wives and two concubines).

Sadly, there was no Joseph at the time some of the tribal divisions in Africa emerged. These conflicts have deep roots that predate present generations and may even predate colonial times. Those who hate other tribes will tell stories that may be hundreds of years old about how the conflict started. What has happened is that the divisions, lack of forgiveness and dysfunctional relationships of one generation have been passed on to the next, and have become part of an entire culture. Children born in that culture have their understandings and perspectives on the world shaped by it. By the time a child is six years old, he or she will know who is to be hated. It is almost as if these ancient conflicts are like a computer operating system that is downloaded into each new generation. What is needed is an "upgraded" operating system, or even better, a totally new operating system that stresses forgiveness and respect rather than hatred and revenge.

Christianity offers a new operating system, but, to continue the computer metaphor, the new system needs to be fully installed if it is to be effective in bringing change. Too often, people are content to rely on "patches" to the old system, rather than fully reconfiguring their cultural programming. What this means in practice is that African Christianity is often very shallow and does not affect the way people live their daily lives. People go to church on Sunday morning, but their lifestyles are influenced more by their culture than by their faith. When culture is the driver, especially if the culture is misaligned with biblical values, it creates an ineffective Christianity that is not much more than nominalism. Forgiveness across tribal lines can only happen when people put Christianity above culture.

It has been said that African self-understanding is first tribal, then national, and finally Christian. This is similar to the way Jonah ranked his priorities. But things should be the other way round: We should first be Christian, then national, and finally tribal. We saw this way of thinking in Joseph when he became an Egyptian leader: his first loyalty was to the Lord; then he served the nation in which he found himself; and finally, he served his father and brothers. This is the sequence we must adopt if we are to be citizens who can move our countries forward. Our Christianity must inform and transform our culture.

Transcending economic barriers

Joseph's godly wisdom and leadership ensured the economic well-being of Egypt and of his own people, the Israelites. Today, we as Christians also have the responsibility and opportunity to demonstrate the right use of economic resources for the good of all. Sadly, we do not always do this well.

I think of an American visitor who had been sending money to support orphans in Zimbabwe. He decided to visit the country and meet the orphans he was sponsoring. He was shocked when he saw that some Christian Zimbabweans enjoyed a far better lifestyle than he did in the USA. He found himself asking why he was sending money when Zimbabwean Christians could be doing this themselves. The gulf between the lifestyles of the rich and the poor in Africa amazed him.

I think, too, of the first time I saw a child living on the street in Harare in the late 1980s. I was deeply troubled by the sight, but it has become all too familiar in recent years. I find myself asking why there are no white children on the streets, but black children are there in abundance. Some would answer that it is because the whites are economically advantaged, but that answer is a little too simplistic.

This situation is even more baffling given the common stereotype that Africans are communal people whereas whites are more individualistic. You would think that our extended families and community-based cultural values would make it impossible to have any child left to live on the street. The very idea should horrify an African mind. And yet it happens, and the situation gets worse and worse while our hearts harden as we pretend not to see it. As the American visitor saw, Africans seem happy to build mansions and live ostentatious lives in the midst of squalor and poverty.

Have you seen any "Nollywood" movies? They accurately depict life in Africa when they show the rich driving into a Hollywood-style mansion, outside whose gates there is a street that looks like a squatter camp. What level of heartlessness does such a scene reveal?

A community with a wide gap between rich and poor is inherently unstable. Sooner or later the poor will rise up and attack the rich. This may take the form of a war of liberation as happened in African countries, or it may be more like the French Revolution in which the people revolted against the rule of the monarchy and aristocrats. Africans rightly rose up and rejected colonial rule because of the oppressive way in which whites ruled; however, it seems that the oppressive leadership style continues, enabling a few to benefit while the masses languish in poverty. Africa has its own aristocrats – people in privileged position in both business and politics. They are thought to be the best among us and it is hoped they will lead diligently. Yet often they do not.

The phenomenon of children on the street is a symptom of the virulent disease of economic inequality. Children growing up deprived while seeing others living in abundance yearn to have what others have, and anger rises against the community that does not seem to care. What is the likely direction of such a child's life? They are at great risk of being drawn into drug addiction, prostitution and violence, becoming a danger to themselves and to society. On the other hand, a child who is given the basics of life – food, shelter, a family and an opportunity to be educated – has a better chance of growing into a useful member of society, benefiting and not harming others. The long-term solution to political violence is to redress the inequalities in society. Most perpetrators of violence are unemployed frustrated young people who have become social dropouts and are willing to harm and maim for a few dollars.

The picture is not all bad though; there are a few glimmers of light and hope on the horizon. A few are doing something about what they see. Orphanages funded and run by Africans are being established. Some business people are coming together to encourage what they call corporate social responsibility, which involves businesses giving back to and helping a community. One African organization that has done this is Econet, which has created various foundations to help thousands of disadvantaged and vulnerable children.

Africa needs more Christian leaders and business people to become heroes of our day, looking after the poor, keeping hospitals going, and doing many other socially beneficial projects. More efforts and initiatives of this kind are needed in all parts of the economy and from more players to redress the situation.

The English saying, "If wishes were horses, beggars would ride" illustrates the difference financial power can make. All humans have their wishes and desires; only those with power can translate their wishes into reality. Joseph had that kind of power; he could do as he wished. Stewards of power realize that they can do what they want with the resources in their charge, and like Joseph they use the power strategically and for the benefit of many. Joseph looked after his whole family – seventy people came from Canaan to Egypt, and Joseph took care of them. Those who are more privileged ought to take care of those who are less privileged. Joseph strategically used his power to provide a piece of land for his family, which he knew, would become a nation.

This is not just a job for a privileged elite, however; it is a job for everyone. The American visitor mentioned earlier represents many ordinary people from that nation and others like it who use what they have to help others. It is they who fund organizations like World Vision because they want to improve the lives of others around the world. This type of attitude contributes to narrowing the gap between rich and poor in their own countries, which in turn brings social stability for all.

Africans traditionally look after their relatives and their children. That is a tradition that needs to continue, but it also needs to be extended so that we also look after those children and adults who have no relatives. As much as possible should be done with the little in the hands of those who believe.

Africa's Religions

Joseph lived in a culture that worshipped the gods of Egypt, yet he remained faithful to his God. He was able to minister to Pharaoh and Egypt without necessarily turning them to his faith. We too live in a multi-religious environment. Some in our nation are Christian, others are Muslim, and others follow African Traditional Religion. What does this mean when it comes to leadership? How should Christians exercise their faith and influence their communities in regions where there are conflicts between those who follow different religions?

Living with Muslims

In recent years, there have been heinous killing and kidnappings of Christians by Islamic extremists. Boko Haram's kidnapping of Christian girls in northern Nigeria, the attack on Westgate Mall in Kenya, the mass killings and beheadings by Al Shabaab and Boko Haram, all done in the name of Islam, seem to cry out for retaliatory action. At times, Christians have indeed responded with violence. In his book *No More Cheeks to Turn?* Sunday Agang reports on some of the violence that Christians in Nigeria have perpetrated in response to Muslim attacks.[6] As he acknowledges, such retaliation can bring Christians down to the same level as the Muslim extremists, and the lines between instigators and victims can become blurred in the ensuing battles between warring factions.

Where religious groups take up arms to further their cause, as is the case with Islamic extremism, state intervention is required to protect innocent civilians. The police and army become involved to combat the militancy of such groups. This level of religious conflict is rightly addressed through national institutions. We will look at the role of such institutions in more detail in chapter seven, where we will look at governance and conflict transformation.

But what should we do as individual Christians? I would argue that we should regard Islamic aggression as persecution for our faith. Christians from antiquity were prepared to die for their faith and not take up arms; these are the foundations of biblical Christianity. Muslims

---

[6] Sunday Agang, *No More Cheeks to Turn?* (Jos: Hippo; Grand Rapids: Zondervan, 2017).

kill for their faith; Christians must be known not for killing but for dying for their faith. Historic events like the crusades are not a reflection of biblical Christianity and should not be repeated.

There is a paradox that the more militant Islam becomes, the more credibility it loses. The deaths of true Christians in the hands of Muslims should not be a reason for individual Christians to take up arms and attack Muslims. It is the role of the state to maintain order and protect citizens. Instead, we should honour those who have died as martyrs in the same way as we honour their predecessors and should continue to reach out in love to our enemies.

One point at which we can reach out to them is by working with those Muslim thinkers who acknowledge that Christianity, Judaism and Islam share some common values since they share an Old Testament faith foundation. These commonalities should be built upon, especially in efforts towards nation building. Those Islamic values which are the same as good biblical values should be encouraged and upheld because they make for wholesome societies. Just as Joseph was prepared to work with a ruler who worshipped different gods to achieve their shared goal of saving the nation from famine, so we too should be prepared to work alongside those who come from other faiths to promote the common good.

As mentioned earlier, Christians are sometimes guilty of sentimentally embracing the person of Christ but not abiding by his principles. When they act like this, they are poor representatives of Christ. Conversely people of Muslim and Jewish faith can embrace the principles but not the person of Christ. They then become people with high ethics, principles and morality, elements that make for wholesome citizens.

Not everyone in our societies will necessarily become Christian, but the biblical values of Christianity are universal.

Living with African Traditional Religion

Christianity's initial interaction with African Traditional Religion (ATR) falls in the category of cultural imperialism. This is what happens when two cultures come into contact and one group uses its economic or military power or its status to promote its own culture and suppress the other. When this happens, the dominated culture often becomes a subculture that is hostile to the stronger culture, waiting for a strategic time to launch an uprising.

During the colonial era, Christianity was introduced as the religion of the dominant culture, and the religion of the subdued African culture became secret and suppressed. Yet because the African belief system and worldview was not altered, adherence to ATR is still strong. It often manifests itself when Africans who are supposedly Christian face a crisis; their default option is to turn to the traditional belief systems for solutions.

The traditional belief system is appeasement focused. It argues that the spirit world needs to be kept happy for life on the earth to function properly. When the spirit world is offended in some way by the behaviour of those on the earth, people's lives are adversely affected. This belief system is also inherently hierarchical. Those who are lower on the scale of authority must give honour and respect to those who are higher on the scale, and must appease them if they are offended in any way, because those higher up have power (ultimately spiritual power) over them. The following diagram illustrates this hierarchy and shows how life is understood in the worldview of ATR.

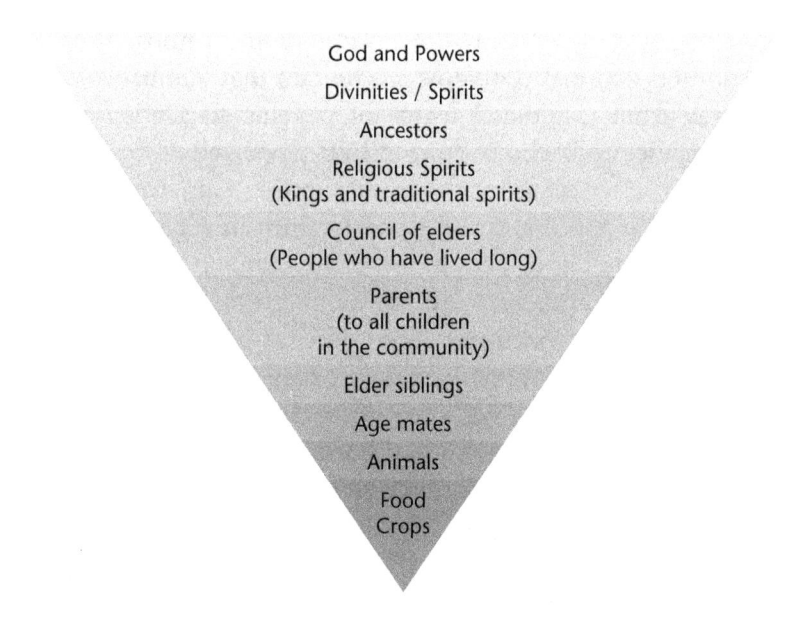

God and Powers
Divinities / Spirits
Ancestors
Religious Spirits
(Kings and traditional spirits)
Council of elders
(People who have lived long)
Parents
(to all children in the community)
Elder siblings
Age mates
Animals
Food
Crops

Figure 2. Power Structure in African Traditional Religion[7]

---

[7] Adapted from a lecture given by Professor Douglas Waruta in September 2013 at International Leadership University, Nairobi, Kenya.

While the soil is at the bottom of the authority scale, it must be understood that all life above it is affected by it and, very importantly, the ancestors are buried in it. Hence the custom of burying the umbilical cord to unite the new-born child with the ancestors who are buried in the soil. The Zimbabwean war of liberation was seen as a kind of holy war forged by the sons of the soil (*mwanawevu*) to re-unite the soil with the departed ancestors who, as shown in the authority scale, are the owners of the land.[8]

In African thinking, people do not die; instead they enter the supernatural realm of the ancestors where they have great influence on events in the natural realm. The world is seen as ultimately spiritual. Nothing happens by accident or coincidence; all events have a spiritual root. Ultimately, everything that happens on the earth derives from the ancestors, spirit powers and gods. Further to this, Africans believe that all power comes from God. Whatever power is exercised on earth comes from God.

As colonial powers have lost their grip on Africa, there has been a strong resurgence of ATR in some places. Some Zimbabwean chiefs have attributed national problems to the fact that Zimbabweans have turned away from traditional forms of worship to Christianity, thus angering the ancestors who now need to be appeased.

To be fully accepted in the African context, Christianity needs to acknowledge that there are some good values in ATR which should not be abandoned. These include the honour shown to elders, *ubuntu* (human kindness), and virginity before marriage. We also need to acknowledge Africa's contributions to and roots in early Christianity. Christianity is not a white man's religion. The Apostle Paul and others took it to Europe from the Middle East in the New Testament period, but two of the three people who sent Barnabas and Saul out in Acts 13 were African. Simeon called Niger was clearly a black man ("niger" is the Latin word for black and became the derogatory term "nigger" in later years) and Lucius of Cyrene. Cyrene was located in present-day Libya and was an ancient centre of Judaism and eventually of the Christian

---

[8] Dwight Simpson, Munyaradzi Mutonono, and Makoto L. Mautsa, "Land", in *Africa Bible Commentary*, ed. Tokunboh Adeyemo (Nairobi, Kenya: WordAlive; Grand Rapids: Zondervan, 2006), 290.

faith, as amply shown by Thomas Oden in his book *The African Memory of Mark: Reassessing Early Church Tradition*.[1]

Above all, we must acknowledge that all cultures ultimately trace their roots to Genesis 11, and that in God's grace all world religions have some elements of truth. In biblical understanding, there is one true God, the creator of heaven and earth. As Africans, we must understand the purest and best of the faith of our fathers as an attempt to relate with this one true God, as all peoples of the earth do. Several similarities in ritual, practice and values can be found between the Old Testament law and ATR.

Joseph had to live in a society that worshipped the gods of Egypt. He was able to minister to Pharaoh and Egypt without necessarily turning them to his faith. In the same way, we need to live in the African context without necessarily turning everyone to our way of believing but demonstrating through our conduct that there is a God whom we follow and that he is the ultimate source of our morality and ethics.

Conclusion

Africans have endured much pain in the past and continue to endure much pain in the present. However, this generation of Africans has been privileged like none before it in its knowledge and understanding of God and in the material comforts with which it has been blessed. The failings of previous generations may be excused because of their ignorance, but this generation stands at a pivotal time in world history. Once again, as it was in the early years of the church, Africa has become a centre of world Christianity. The quality of African Christianity is thus key to the face of Christianity in this generation. Forgiveness and reconciliation in the areas of race, tribe, economics and religion are essential if Christianity is to achieve its goals on the African continent.

Joseph was able to rise above race and tribe, forgiving his brothers and effecting reconciliation. He used the economic resources that God gave him for the benefit of all and lived in a pluralistic religious

---

[1] Thomas Oden, *The African Memory of Mark: Reassessing Early Church Tradition* (Downers Grove: IVP Academic, 2011).

environment as a true representative of God in his generation, African Christians should strive to do the same.

For Discussion

1. Alexander Pope wrote, "to err is human, to forgive divine". Joseph forgave his brothers because of the godly character that had been worked into him. On the other hand, Jonah, though he sincerely loved the Lord and was devoted to him, could not forgive the Assyrians. Can people who have no knowledge of God truly forgive? Do Christians have an advantage over non-Christians when it comes to extending forgiveness?
2. How does an appreciation of one's blessings make one disposed to show kindness, compassion and forgiveness? On the other hand, how does a bitter heart affect the behaviour of someone who had been wronged?
3. Pain inflicted through racism, tribalism, economic oppression and religious intolerance can cause a root of bitterness to grow in the heart. How can a person who has been victimized in this way let go of the bitterness?
4. After suffering life's injustices, do you now have a Jonah heart or a Joseph heart?

6

MORALITY AND INTEGRITY

Morality and integrity were key elements in Joseph's life and leadership. They are the pillars necessary to build a church that is worthy of its calling in Africa. But before we look at their role in Africa, it may be helpful to define these terms in a little more detail.

Defining Terms

Ethics and morality are closely related, but are not identical. Ethics refers to a code of conduct that is external to the individual. As believers, our ethics are determined by the character of God and by his pronouncements about what is right and good, and what is wrong and bad. Our morality, however, is more internal and reflects what we actually value as right or wrong. When we are in a right relationship with God, we both understand that God is the one who says what is right and wrong and we show by our lives that we agree with what God says.

Integrity is a measure of the distance between a person's internal values and their public image. A person who has low integrity knows what type of behaviour is expected by God or by society (in other words, they are aware of ethical standards) and conforms to them when others are watching, but when alone does whatever suits their own moral standards. That is why it is possible to be ethical in conduct but immoral in heart. The English saying, "all that glitters is not gold", captures the idea that what is inside may not match the outside. That should not be true of believers, for they should be people of high integrity.

As Christian believers, we should be striving to be like God. The more our ethics and morality are aligned with his, the more we reflect God's image. But if we do not align our values with his, we will convey a distorted view of his image. The greater the misalignment, the greater the distortion and twistedness of the reflected image. That is a frightening prospect – we should dread the very possibility of being charged with misrepresenting God!

Holistic Thinking

Delanyo Adadevoh's book *Moral Vision and Nation Building* begins by pointing to the great aspirations and ambitions embodied in the national plans of various countries. These plans, he says, tend to focus on economics, science and technology:

> What is sadly missing in all these plans is the forgotten foundational element in all human development, which is the character and morality we desire for our future. The economic, scientific and technological development goals all address what we want our nations and people to have in the future. These goals include good roads, industries, strong economies and scientific breakthroughs ... What many of the leaders of this century are not addressing is the fundamental question about the kind of people we want to become in the future. What is lacking in our plans for the future is a moral vision. Ironically, the issues of character and morality have a direct bearing on economic and technological development.[2]

Adadevoh then goes on to argue for a holistic approach to nation building that addresses moral values too. He identifies eleven values that need to be cultivated, namely, God-centredness, a sense of the sacredness of human life, positive self-identity, personal and public integrity, a sense of community (communality), empowering leadership, justice, freedom, productivity, maximization and excellence.

---

[2] Delanyo Adadevoh, *Moral Vision and Nation Building* (Orlando, FL: International Leadership Foundation, 2010), 1.

Adadevoh's insights push us to move beyond common thinking about the role of the church in society, which is too often restricted to getting people into the church building. He urges us to set out to permeate the whole of society with the Bible-based moral values listed above, arguing that these values can be infused into African society without necessarily demanding conversion to the Christian faith. Some might indeed be converted to the faith after meeting believers who uphold these high moral ideals, but that is not essential provided we can agree on the moral and ethical values required to guide the transformation of the continent. Not everyone in Western society became a Christian, even when Christianity was at its most influential. To expect everyone in Africa to become a Christian is unrealistic. But by teaching and practising holistic moral values, Christian principles can become the norm in society.

The values listed above are also not unique to Christianity but are shared by other religions. After all, religion is closely connected with the moral and ethical values of all people. So, in working to bring about societal transformation, we must work with those of other faiths. This is easier than some might think, for Africans are religious and most worship God in some form or another. Secularism is far less common than in the Western world. We are agreed that God is at the centre of everything, even though we may disagree about who this God is, and we can come together around the values that are needed to transform our societies for the better.

Now what we need are the leaders who can take us along this path to transformation.

Christian Leadership

While Muslims and traditionalists can be leaders in society, my concern in this book is with the Christian contribution. Do we have African Christian leaders who are credible, dependable, and trusted both in the church and in society? Only if we can offer godly leaders of proven integrity can we as Christians make a positive contribution to the transformation of Africa.

The fundamentals: character, integrity and credibility

As we saw in chapter three, Joseph was entrusted with leadership responsibilities because of his integrity, which was rooted in his faith in God. Things have not changed in the centuries since then, and issues of character and morality are still foundational to biblical leadership in any area of life. Christian leaders who show godly character and morality that has been tested (integrity) are best placed to become, credible, dependable and trusted leaders, as the following diagram shows.

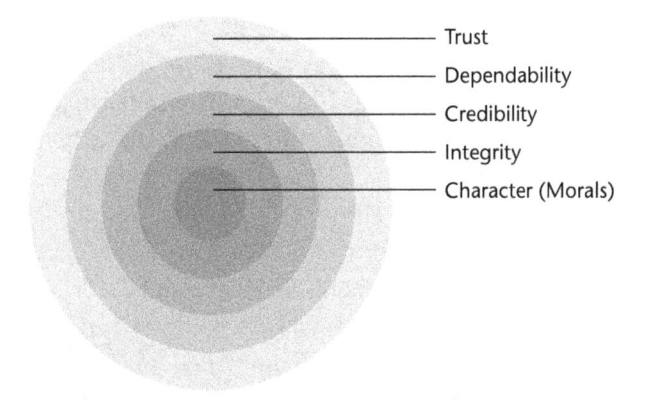

- Trust
- Dependability
- Credibility
- Integrity
- Character (Morals)

Figure 3. From Character to Trust

The most effective leaders are those whom people willingly follow. Through persuasion they convince people and thereby create movements. The lowest form of leadership is by coercion (force). While it is possible to achieve some victories through coercive means, these victories do not last. Sooner or later those controlled by force of any kind – whether it be imperialistic, military, economic or any other force – will rise up and resist their oppressors. Wise leaders know that human beings operate best when they freely make decisions.

People learn more from what leaders do than from what they say. Jesus spent three years in close proximity with his disciples before he sent them out. Those three years would have enabled them to see him walk the talk. His actions were consistent with his message, for his integrity was an important part of the discipleship process. Biblical discipleship is life-on-life interaction. Leaders model godliness, they do not just teach it as abstract theory; their character is at the core of the process. That is why the Apostle Paul said, "Follow my example as I follow the example of Christ." (1 Cor 11:1). Similarly, in another very profound statement that illustrates the importance of the relationship between character, integrity and credibility, he said, "Whatever you have learned or received or heard from me, or seen in me – put it into practice. And the God of peace will be with you" (Phil 4:9).

But what characteristics attract people and make them willing to follow a leader? Two American researchers set out to answer this question.[3] They asked thousands of people all over the world "What values (personal traits or characteristics) do you look for and admire in your leader?"

They found that the four characteristics that more than half their respondents favoured were being honest, forward-looking, competent and inspiring. It is interesting that these qualities are evident in the life of the biblical Joseph. His honesty or integrity caused him to be trusted by all he worked with; his stewardship skills, especially in his administration of Egypt, illustrate what a forward-looking leader does. After interpreting Pharaoh's dream, he proposed a fourteen-year strategic plan for Egypt, and was given the responsibility of implementing it. His competency was clear: Potiphar and the jail authorities had recognized it, and so did Pharaoh, who was inspired by Joseph, saying, "Can we find a man like this, in whom is the spirit of God?"

Kouzes and Posner also asked people to list seven characteristics of a leader they would *willingly* follow. They found that 88 percent of respondents listed honesty as one of the seven characteristics. It scored higher than all the other qualities. This shows that people want leaders they can trust. Untrustworthy leaders leave people feeling cheated and lied to.

Credibility is thus at the core of leadership. This is why leaders' private lives matter. For example, if a man cheats in his marriage, the closest and most intimate relationship he can have, he is more likely to cheat in other spheres such as his work or business. People will judge that he is probably less trustworthy than a person who remains faithful to his wife. If we looked more closely at people's private lives, perhaps public life disasters would be less frequent.

---

[3] James Kouzes and Barry Posner, *The Leadership Challenge* (San Francisco: Josey Bass, 2002), 24.

How do we judge people's honesty in the public sphere? One way is to look at their integrity over time. All political leaders at all levels of government try to convince their constituents that they have their best interests at heart, but their credibility is best judged a few years after they gain political office. Then the gap between what they said and what they have done becomes apparent.

We could think of this in terms of the way gold is assayed by putting it in a furnace. At room temperature, one piece of gold looks much like another. However, when the pieces are put through the furnace, it becomes clear which piece contains impurities and which does not.

The fire in which a person's integrity or the quality of their character is tested is life itself – as we saw with Joseph. There is a common saying that money, sex and power bring out the best and worst in people. How many men will say no to a woman who offers herself to them? How much money is enough money? How many people in authority think first of the trust they have been given before enjoying the privileges that come with the office? Many executives want a corner office, an executive car (preferably the latest Mercedes-Benz), a fat salary and all manner of perks. By the time they leave, the company is often in a worse position than they found it. They are motivated solely by a selfish agenda and scoff at the idea of helping make life better for society and providing jobs that will enhance the lives of others.

Such people have failed the test of integrity. Integrity is tough. It asks deep questions. It examines values and motives. It wants to know who you really are and what you are really about.

Public office is particularly demanding in this regard. Those who are given public office are entrusted with the livelihoods and future of their constituents. They manage the country's resources on their behalf. Thus it is vital that they be people of the highest integrity. If they are not, it is like asking a wolf to guard lambs. It is leaders who lack integrity who have been plundering Africa's natural resources, its diamonds, gold, platinum and uranium, and using them for their own enrichment rather than for the benefit of all.

Africa's future depends on the calibre of our leaders. We are endowed with great resources and there is no need for us to languish in poverty. We need leaders we can believe in, who uphold high standards of integrity and whose characters are solid. We need leaders who will not take anything from anyone unless they obtain it legitimately. We need leaders who truly seek to improve the lives of those they lead, who are not primarily motivated by personal gain but genuinely work to make everyone's life better.

While all in public office may not be Christians, they should all be expected to have a high level of ethics and morality. It should be demanded of them. Leaders should be people of high integrity; people who inspire us to high ideals.

This is not to say that those who lead should be perfect, for no human being is perfect. But there is a great difference between someone who is basically a person of integrity and someone of questionable character. The stakes are too high for us to entrust our riches, livelihood and futures to people we do not trust.

As Dr Kwegir Aggrey, the first African vice-principal of Achimota College, Ghana once said, "Only the best is good enough for Africa."[4] We want the best, and only the best we have, to lead us; the stakes are too high to settle for anything less.

Sober leadership

Intelligence and gifting have opened the way for many who aspire to leadership. But these qualities are not enough, even when combined with integrity. The best leaders are those who have also learned self-control. Such leaders are not emotionally driven but take time to think about all sides of an important issue before coming to a decision. When important decisions are made in haste or anger, the consequences can be disastrous, especially if the decision maker is opinionated, stubborn, has a large ego and will not listen to other points of view or back down when he or she realizes that there is a flaw in their thinking.

Nations have spent years in the wilderness of economic and political chaos because of decisions that were not well thought through. This is particularly true in Africa, where in their euphoria at the departure of a hard taskmaster people fail to think strategically. Decisions are made in an emotional mixture of joy, anger, and lust for retribution. African history is full of political leaders who came into office and immediately expelled anyone they viewed as working in collusion with their oppressor or enemy.

---

[4] Adadevoh, *Personal Life Transformation*, 47–49, 71.

We could understand if Joseph had acted like this. But by God's grace, Joseph was able to get over the bitterness of past hurts. He did not give in to seething anger and seize the opportunity to take revenge. He was a wise and forgiving man who had become bigger than the petty jealousies of childhood. He was a national leader, thinking about the future of millions, and seeing far into the purposes of God for the infantile nation of Israel.

We too should seek leaders who will act with Christian maturity. The Apostle Paul gives us an indication of what that looks like when he sets outs the character-based qualities that should guide the selection of leaders: They should be blameless and (or above reproach), the husband of one wife, sober (or temperate), self-controlled, respectable, not given to drunkenness, not violent but gentle, not quarrelsome, not a lover of money (1 Tim 3:2–3). These qualities are important not only for church leaders, but for all Christian leaders. They constitute a plumb line or standard for their behaviour.

If I were to try to summarize all the biblical qualities of leadership mentioned above I would do so using one word: "sober". Sober leaders will think through the implications of decisions before rushing into them. They will encourage rational, long-term planning that is clearly and logically communicated. They will discourage the type of emotionally charged environments that foster irrational or illogical decision-making and create a toxic leadership environment.

China offers us an example of what such planning looks like. It is on the way to becoming a dominant world power and has a very clearly laid out plan of development that is communicated to its citizens. For example, there are plans for the development of Beijing over the next thirty years, and a model of the future city is in place so that people can see where they are headed. The leaders are taking concrete, measurable steps towards the accomplishment of this vision. Is there any such plan for an African city?

An African example of long-term thinking is Botswana. This is a country whose main sources of income are its diamond deposits. In many places, the wealth these generate would benefit only the rich, but the Botswana government has taken steps to ensure that the poorest and the weakest in the country are also benefiting. Every Motswana child has a right to attend school, at the government's expense. And at school, the children are given food, so that hunger does not interfere with their learning. If a child shows aptitude, the government will also pay for their university education. The country is using its wealth to invest in its future.

Botswana has not escaped the HIV/AIDs epidemic that has ravaged Africa. But it has set up a plan that makes antiretroviral drugs (ARVs) freely available to all who need them. They even have a social services network strong enough to provide food for those who apply and are approved for it.

While other African countries boast of all kinds of natural resources, they seem to have no clear long-term plan or strategy for their use. How will these resources be translated into wealth in the hands of the people and how will they change the lives of citizens? In the absence of clear plans and policies, human selfishness takes over and those who have access to the resources plunder them, taking all they can and using it to support an extravagant lifestyle, without regard for anyone else. In the absence of clear plans and policies, natural resources become a curse instead of a blessing. They encourage the unscrupulous to maintain the status quo of chaos and bad governance because it works to their advantage, while the rest of the country suffers.

Sober, disciplined leaders are not concerned to enrich themselves but focus on mapping out clear strategies to build their nations. Their goal is not personal wealth but enabling all Africans to lead a dignified life. Pensioners need to be taken care of, young people need jobs – why should they be educated to work for other nations? Good quality health care should be accessible for all. Good housing, clean water, electricity and all the amenities of modern life should be available to all. Instead of a legacy of greed, sober leaders will leave a legacy of functioning countries where all can prosper.

Where can we find such sober leaders? Can we find them in our churches? We need to seek out and encourage godly leaders who have character, integrity and credibility. And the only way to develop such leaders is to constantly stress the importance of seeking to grow to maturity in Christ and living Spirit-controlled lives. Only then will we see sober, credible Christian leaders who can be entrusted with leadership of the continent.

The State of the African Church

In order to be able to lead transformation on the continent, the church needs to model character, integrity and credibility in local congregations throughout the continent. When it does this, society will look to the church for leadership.

Note that when I say "the church" I am not referring to any building or institution, but to the people of God. Wherever God's people are found, that is the church, the *ekklesia*, the people who have been called out of the world to serve the world. All over the world, the church gathers for a few hours on Sunday, and then the church scatters (there is a diaspora of the church every Sunday) and goes to the various places in which Christians live out their faith.

The extent to which the gathered church models leadership to its members is the extent to which the scattered church can do the same in society at large. So be it in business, politics, education, health, industry, agriculture or any other sector of society, wherever a Christian is, the church is. The church is called to be the salt of the earth and the light of the world, stopping the rot and showing the way to the world. As Joseph was a model of morality and integrity wherever he went and so was entrusted with leadership, so the African church should be a model to the world.

Africa has many examples of faithful followers of Christ who ought to be emulated. They are quietly influencing their communities in positive and godly ways. Yet in recent years, we have seen leadership practices in the gathered African church moving away from those set out in the Bible. Today, the voice that often speaks loudest is boastful and propagates values that are difficult to reconcile with biblical teaching and example. True, such leaders insist that they have biblical precedent for what they do, but we need to check whether they are following biblical precedents or biblical principles. Precedents merely tell us what happened in a given situation; principles tell us what should happen. For example, we have biblical precedent for polygamy, but the Bible makes it plain that the biblical principle for marriage is monogamy. In the church context, we have biblical precedent for gathering in homes; the biblical principle, however, is that believers need to meet together regularly, whether in a home or in some other building. Thus, a precedent may or may not be a guide to how we should behave. It is important that church traditions and practices be critiqued in light of biblical principles – what the Bible actually teaches.

The Bible is our standard, and any deviation from its original intent is a deviation from God's revealed standard. God had and still has a way in which he wants his church to be led. So we must be ready to critique both modern and traditional church practices in light of biblical revelation, because when church practice is aligned to biblical teaching, the church models the way to the world.

The problem of anarchy

The African church, especially in its evangelical and Pentecostal/charismatic expressions, suffers from a serious lack of accountability structures. We see this in the proliferation of breakaway groups led by self-appointed leaders who call themselves apostles, prophets, or bishops and welcome honorifics like "man of God", "the anointed of God", "father" or "papa". Some even expect people to kneel in their presence and to treat their words as the words of God himself. They demand loyalty and obedience from their followers, and anyone who questions anything they do is accused of opposing God. The atmosphere is cult-like.

Even in more established churches we see a disturbing lack of accountability. For example, some Christian leaders have experienced such serious marital problems that they have sought divorce, yet they continue in ministry. Or we encounter situations where nobody asks questions about church finances and any gift to the church is treated as the personal property of the man or woman of God. Nobody questions the ethics of how money is obtained from church members, and there is no tolerance for questions about how the money is used.

The result is an atmosphere of anarchy. Leaders do as they please, insisting that they are accountable to nobody but God because God has uniquely called and gifted them, making them different from ordinary mortals who might question their conduct.

The diagram below illustrates the kind of toxic leadership I have been talking about. It begins with a self-appointed leader who is accountable to no human authority. This person starts a church movement that people regard as "powerful" because of the leader's eloquent preaching or exciting miracles. The more people who are attracted to this movement, the more powerful the leader becomes until he is perceived as an untouchable, a "man of God" who must be obeyed without question. Such a leader keeps at a distance from his flock. When he appears in public, he is surrounded by bodyguards. His followers have to seek an appointment if they hope to speak with him. The result is a toxic environment that is very different from what a church environment should be.

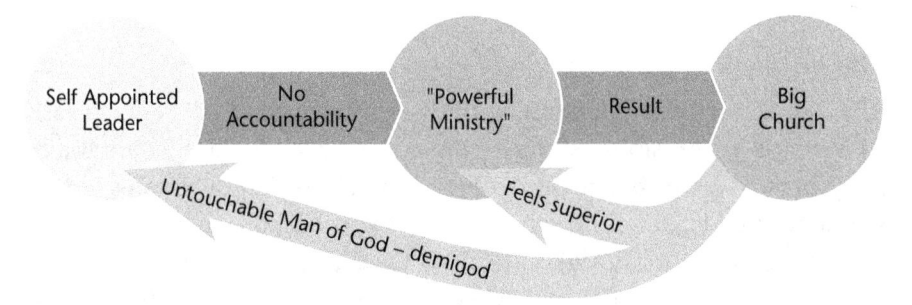

Figure 4. Toxic Faith

The basis for leadership

What are we to make of the argument that a leader of a contemporary church was given gifts by God, and ordained or appointed by God, so that he or she is not answerable to any human authority? We need to respond by pointing to the biblical principles for the appointment of church leaders. When we look at the New Testament, we see that the qualification for leadership is not gifting and calling but a Christ-like character. Look again at Paul's words to Timothy:

> Now the overseer must be above reproach, the husband of but one wife, temperate, self-controlled, respectable, hospitable, able to teach, not given to drunkenness, not violent but gentle, not quarrelsome, not a lover of money. He must manage his own family well and see that his children obey him with proper respect ... He must not be a recent convert, or he may become conceited and fall under the same judgement as the devil. (1 Tim 3:1–6)

Timothy was to select leaders for the church based on these criteria. New Testament leaders did not appoint themselves; they were appointed based on qualifications that reflected the Christlikeness of their character. Character is important because a leader does not teach by word only, but by what he or she says and does. Often, the teaching is more by deed than word.

Notice that there is no mention of calling or gifting here; the qualification is purely character based: how much is this potential leader like Christ? This is not to underplay the value of spiritual gifts or to say that spiritual gifts are unnecessary in the church. But spiritual gifts, especially spectacular gifts that attract attention, should be accompanied by abundant evidence of a godly character. Where such character is lacking, we may well question the source of the gift.

When the church is led by godly, mature Christian leaders, its foundations are solid. But when the leadership is immature, or even ungodly, the church is fragile, unreliable and unstable. It fails to model good leadership to the world, and it will not produce good leaders to serve the world.

The role of prophecy and miracles

If character is the key qualification for leadership, what is the place of gifts of prophecy and healing in the church and in society? What are we to make of the fact that prophets are paid much attention in Africa and speak not only to the church but also make political pronouncements and predictions? What a prophet says in a church meeting about a president or the socio-political environment is taken very seriously, to the extent of getting wide media coverage. Is this not a sign of leadership?

It is true that prophets are honoured in Africa. This tradition has a long history, dating back to the African shamans who were believed to have access to the spirit world and so were called on to give guidance to traditional leaders and society in general. In traditional African society, exercising spiritual power was proof of shamanistic abilities. The more power demonstrated, the stronger the shamanistic abilities and the greater the attention given to the shaman. Predictive prophecy is therefore highly valued because it draws attention to the prophet who has replaced the traditional shaman but operates in much the same way and is respected as a spiritual guide.

The New Testament, however, warns us to be cautious when it comes to assuming that supernatural gifts are a basis for appointing someone as a leader. Gifts may be deceptive and may not come from God. As Paul warns us, "The coming of the lawless one will be in accordance with the work of Satan displayed in all kinds of counterfeit miracles, signs and wonders, and in every sort of evil that deceives those who are perishing" (2 Thess 2:9–10). Notice that the issue of lawlessness identifies or characterizes the works of Satan.

Jesus also warned us against false prophets:

> Watch out for false prophets. They come to you in sheep's clothing, but inwardly they are ferocious wolves. By their fruit you will recognize them. Do people pick grapes from thornbushes, or figs from thistles? Likewise, every good tree bears good fruit, but a bad tree bears bad fruit. A good tree cannot bear bad fruit, and a bad tree cannot bear good fruit. Every tree that does not bear good fruit is cut down and thrown into the fire. Thus, by their fruit you will recognize them... . Many will say to me on that day, "Lord, Lord, did we not prophesy in your name and in your name drive out demons and in your name perform many miracles?" Then I will tell them plainly, "I never knew you. Away from me, you evildoers!" (Matt 7:15–23)

From God's perspective, the fruit is more important than the gifts. What really matters is the prophet's character. The gifts are not ends in themselves; they are means to an end. They confirm the work of God through a given leader and point people to God who is the giver of the gifts. If the leader's character is not godly, the gifts count for nothing.

The other point that we should note is that it is not just the prophets and miracle workers who have received gifts from God; so have all those who follow Jesus. Not all of these gifts are awe-inspiring; some are manifested in humble service to others. But they are nonetheless gifts of the Spirit, which God apportions as he wills. This is the important point that Peter made in his sermon on the day of Pentecost, when he pointed to the fulfilment of the Old Testament Scripture, "I will pour out my Spirit on all people" (Acts 2:17).

Peter's point was that what was happening in his day was very different from what had happened in Old Testament times when only prophets, priests and kings were specially anointed and ordained for ministry. They would have the Spirit fall on them and would speak on God's behalf. The rest of the people would not have the Spirit and would be instructed by the anointed man of God. So the man of God was someone who was specially called out by God. But in the New Testament, the phrase "man of God" refers to believers in general (see 2 Tim 3:17, where the words translated "servant of God" in the NIV should literally be translated "man of God" as in the ESV and KJV). All believers are now men and women of God, and none can claim this title for himself.

Since prophecy is so important in Africa and since it affects all society, not just the church, it is important to be clear about how biblical prophecy works, especially in the New Testament. The following table contrasts the Old Testament way of receiving prophecy with the New Testament way:

Prophecy in the Old Testament	Prophecy in the New Testament
Spirit comes upon one special man of God	Spirit falls on all flesh
Prophet hears from God and tells the people what he has heard	The veil is torn and all have access to holy of holies. Anyone can hear from God
Prophecy to be obeyed	Prophecy to be tested first
Kings, prophets and priests (special men of God)	The priesthood of all believers. All can be used by God as priests and prophets

Table 1 Comparison of the Prophetic Role in the Old and New Testaments

A very important aspect of this comparison concerns how recipients of prophecy should receive a prophetic word. The general tendency in Africa is to obey everything that a "man of God" says. In the Old Testament, a prophet would be obeyed until what he predicted did not come to pass (Deut 18:17–22), but in the New Testament the correct response to prophecy is to evaluate what is said before obeying it. Every prophecy must be tested to see if it is in line with biblical truth (1 Thess 5:20–21).

Another common mistake people make involves the meaning of the word "prophecy". Biblical prophecy is not so about much foretelling the future as it is about forth-telling, that is, speaking to today's situations on God's behalf. The primary intent of the prophets was not to predict the future but to speak for God. Today's prophets make prediction the main issue, some even offering online prophecies and predicting soccer results. They are little more than fortune-tellers, aiming to impress and mesmerize, but not to bring people closer to God.

We see similar misunderstandings in regard to miracles. While it is true that God sometimes acts supernaturally, the miracle itself is not the main issue. The important thing is what the miracle points to. Miracles are intended to serve God's agenda by bringing him glory and honour and extending his kingdom. Jack Deere makes this point well:

> One clear purpose of miracles was to authenticate the character of Jesus and his relationship with his heavenly Father. In this regard, miracles demonstrate the following: God is with Jesus (John 3:2); Jesus is from God (John 3:2; 9:32-33); God has sent Jesus (John 5:36); Jesus has authority on earth to forgive sins (Mark 2:10-11; Matt 9:6-7; Luke 5:24-25); Jesus is approved by God (Acts 2:22); the Father is in Jesus and Jesus is in the Father (John 10:37-38; 14:11); in Jesus the kingdom of God has come (Matt 12:28; Luke 11:20); and Jesus is the Messiah (Matt 11:1-6; Luke 7:18-23) and the Son of God (Matt 14:25-33).
>
> A second purpose of miracles was to authenticate the message about Jesus. This was the major function of the miracles as far as the ministry of the apostles was concerned. In Mark 16:20 and Acts 14:3 – notice that in both of these texts the Lord does not confirm the apostles themselves but rather "his word" or "the message" that the apostles were preaching. Signs and wonders do not testify to the apostles but to the message of salvation preached by the apostles. So the two principal things that are authenticated by miracles are the Lord Jesus and the message about the Lord Jesus.... miracles do not authenticate the apostles! And if we think about the theology of the New Testament, this makes perfect sense. With

the coming of Jesus Christ, God wants all attention directly to his Son. The primary task of the Holy Spirit is to exalt Jesus Christ. God is not interested in bearing witness to his servants but rather to his Son and the message about his Son.[5]

Today, however, miracles are often treated as the main issue, and the ability to perform miracles is seen as the ultimate test of a leader's competency. Those who do not perform miracles are regarded as useless and impotent, while those who do are seen as powerful and as the legitimate leaders of the church.

As regards prophecy and miracles, the African church is not modelling the way for our society; it is instead becoming a cesspool of shamanistic behaviours which mislead rather than bless people.

Titles, hierarchy and power-distance

African leaders love titles. All manner of accolades and titles would be given to kings and leaders of old. Praise singers would announce their arrival with innumerable flattering metaphors. Idi Amin, the former Ugandan president, is said to have given himself the following titles: "His Excellency, Field Marshall, Al-Haji, Dr. Idi Amin Dada, Life President of Uganda, conqueror of the British Empire, distinguished service order of the Military Cross, Victoria Cross and Professor of Geography." Such titles serve to set the leader apart from all others, creating a distance between him or her and the rest of the people. It is the same desire for superiority that drives contemporary leaders to anoint themselves as apostles and prophets and bishops and archbishops. They want others to see them as a special class of Christians, and to accept their status in a hierarchy of power and control.

This love of titles is not unique to African culture; it is very much present in European culture too, with its kings and princes, dukes and lords. It is also present in traditional church culture, where leaders' titles vary according to their hierarchical status. So the terms Reverend, Right Reverend, Very Reverend, Most Reverend, His Grace and the like are used for priests, bishops, archbishops, cardinals and the pope.

---

[5] Jack Deere, *Surprised by the Power of the Spirit* (Eastbourne: Kingsway, 1994), 103–104.

No such hierarchical structure was found in the original church. The New Testament makes it clear that there was plurality of leadership and mutual accountability among the elders and apostles. The word "apostle" did not show status in terms of hierarchical rank; rather, it denoted a person's function as someone who had been sent. The apostles had been sent out to plant and establish churches. Once they had done this, they would appoint a group of elders to oversee each congregation. Within this leadership, the apostles were content to refer to themselves as fellow elders (1 Pet 5:3; 2 John 1; 3 John 1), and they would honour and submit to the local leaders when they were in their region. This is why Paul was free to rebuke Peter publically when he saw Peter leading the whole church astray in Galatia (Gal 2:11–21).

It was only after the first century that a hierarchy developed, with a single bishop overseeing several churches. Eventually this became the official norm: "After his conversion (AD 312) Constantine appointed bishops as civil magistrates throughout the empire, organized the church into dioceses along the pattern of Roman regional districts, and consistently used 'clerical' and 'clerics' as a privileged class."[6]

Constantine influenced the church to adopt a strong hierarchy. Eventually, the pope came to rival and even surpass the emperor in privileges and power. Christian leaders ceased to be servants and became masters. The pattern is illustrated in the diagram below.

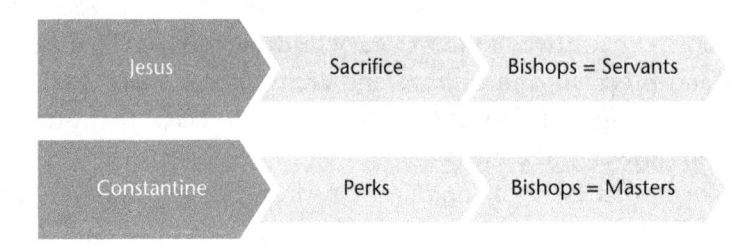

Jesus	Sacrifice	Bishops = Servants
Constantine	Perks	Bishops = Masters

Figure 5. Servants Becoming Masters

This movement to a strong hierarchy and control continues today, although we may no longer think in terms of princes. Instead, modern leaders are more like superstars, pop-idols, and movie actors, with the lifestyles to match.

---

[6] R. Paul Stevens, *The Other Six Days* (Grand Rapids: Eerdmans, 1999), 44.

What has become of the model of leadership that Christ taught, where he described leadership using the metaphors of a shepherd or servant or steward? How can we expect to see servant leaders in society when we do not see them in our churches?

Reflection

Joseph set a good example of leadership; many current leaders in the church in Africa are setting bad ones. Instead of acting as role models, they act like characters in a soap opera. They offer a parody of leadership that undermines the church's credibility. If the African church is to rise to the challenge of leading and discipling the nation, we need to provide an example of how to govern.

Shallow understandings of biblical leadership combined with years of ungodly leadership traditions, both African and European, have influenced the church. Though he lived thousands of years ago, Constantine is very much with us today; his spirit prevails in many of today's church structures. When this is combined with traditional African propensities to flattering titles and hero-worship, we have the makings of a chaotic leadership structure. Issues of character, qualifications, accountability, submission and fellowship seem not to be regarded highly anymore. We need to reclaim them.

It is striking that even the Apostle Paul, who was called by Jesus himself, saw Jesus and was taught by him directly, would not go ahead and preach without the approval and blessing of the other apostles (Gal 1:11–2:10). Is there a lesson in that for us?

It is time to stop our childish church politics and become the kind of leaders who will maturely shepherd our generation. The church needs to self-regulate or rather, like Joseph, it needs to fear God above anything else and not wait for national government structures to do the regulating. We should be providing an example and leading the world, but if something does not change we are in such a sorry state that the world will have to bring order in the church, if that is possible.

For Discussion

1. Do you agree that the African church often lacks integrity and morality and so has lost credibility and the ability to speak authoritatively to society? If so, why? If not, why not?
2. If it is true that credibility has been lost, what can be done to regain it?
3. What emotions do followers experience when under the coercive leadership of a leader they do not admire? Conversely, what emotions do they experience under a persuasive leader that they do admire?
4. The church needs to be revived so that the nation can be awakened. Discuss.

7

STEWARDSHIP AND POWER

The Message, a paraphrase of the Bible, is very good at bringing out God's intention when he created human beings:

> God spoke: "Let us make human beings in our image, make them reflecting our nature so they can be responsible for the fish in the sea, the birds in the air, the cattle, and, yes, Earth itself, and every animal that moves on the face of Earth." God created human beings; he created them godlike, reflecting God's nature. He created them male and female. God blessed them: "Prosper! Reproduce! Fill the Earth! Take charge! Be responsible for fish in the sea and birds in the air, for every living thing that moves on the face of Earth." (Gen 1:26–28, MSG)

Theologians refer to these words as humanity's "cultural mandate". It is also a call to stewardship, which for our purposes I will treat as meaning "management". The point being made is that God is the creator and owner of everything in the universe and that he gives us our lives and the responsibility to manage everything he has created. You own nothing, not even the breath you are taking as you read this. God gives us everything and entrusts us with the earth. Nothing about this mandate has changed since it was first given to us. We are still called to be stewards of all that God has given us.

In the first part of this book, we saw how Jonah and Joseph practised stewardship. They used what God had given them – their personal knowledge of him, their relationships and the abilities – to impact and influence whole nations in their generation.

Today, evangelical Christianity rightly emphasizes Matthew 28:18–20, which is also called the Great Commission or discipleship mandate. It focuses our attention on making disciples. But we should not forget the mandate of Genesis 1:26–28. When we go out to make disciples, we are told to teach them "to obey everything I have commanded you" (Matt 28:20) – and that includes the command in Genesis.

To come at this from another angle, we can say that the goal of the discipleship mandate is to produce mature disciples, or as Paul puts it, to attain "the whole measure of the fullness of Christ" (Eph 4:12). In other words, mature believers should be like Christ. As we become like him, we shall increasingly manifest the image of God and we will increasingly work to fulfil the cultural mandate to make responsible use of the resources that God has given us.

It is not too much to say that God holds mature Christians responsible for the state of creation. He expects us to be the creators of culture, specifically God-inspired culture. He expects us to do so using the resources he gives. Thus, we need to stop thinking about stewardship solely in terms of the management of church resources; it is much more, it is the management of God's creation.

It is also worth taking time to look at the word translated "take charge" in *The Message* or "subdue" in earlier translations of the Bible.

> The term "subdue" (Hb. *kabash*) elsewhere means to bring a people or land into subjection so that it will yield service to the one subduing it (Num 32:22, 29). Here the idea is that the man and woman are to make the earth's resources beneficial for themselves, which implies that they would investigate and develop the earth's resources to make them useful for human beings generally. This command provides a foundation for wise scientific and technological development; the evil uses to which people have put their dominion come as a result of Genesis 3.[1]

Traditional churches have maintained the geographical thinking that is behind both the Great Commission (to make disciples of all nations – that is, all people groups, tribes and ethnicities) and the creation mandate (to subdue all the earth). Traditional churches, like churches in the

---

[1] *English Standard Version Study Bible* (Wheaton, IL: Crossway, 2008), 52.

Bible, think geographically. In the Bible, there is the church in Ephesus, the church in Antioch, the church in Jerusalem, the church in Rome and so on. The church is always geographically located, and from that geographical location believers go outside the church building to affect the world around, extending God's dominion or kingdom as they do so. Traditional churches have changed the communities and environments they touched. When a mission station was established, not only would a church building be put up but also a school and hospital. The basic necessities of life like clean water would be made accessible through the church to the community.

The more modern evangelical and Pentecostal/charismatic churches in Africa tend to be more individualistic in their thinking. Church amounts to not much more than a "bless me" club. Congregants want to be personally blessed, and once they receive the blessings, they enjoy them with their families, living beautiful comfortable lives. Instead of seeking to change the communities they are in, people move from one community to another seeking a more powerful church that will enable them to have more of the sought-after breakthroughs and blessings. This may be one reason why the African church seems to be ineffective in societal transformation even though the numbers of adherents continue to grow.

Stewardship, Power and Resources

Power is something that is often misunderstood. Some long for it; others speak as if it is dirty and undesirable. We associate it with high office or great wealth. What we fail to recognize is that almost all people exercise power in one form or another. Not all of us are Josephs who lead nations or Jonahs who prophesy to entire cities. But most of us have some power – even if it is only the power that comes from having greater economic resources than someone else. Or we may have social power because we are well-regarded in our communities. We also hold electoral power – those who hold political office know that they owe their position to the people who voted for them, who can also vote against them. I am conscious that I hold power as I write this book because those who read it may be affected by it. So, what are we to do with all this power?

A biblical understanding of power is contained in the word "stewardship". A steward is someone who exercises power on behalf of someone else. A steward's power is not self-derived but is entrusted to them by one who is far more powerful. As human beings, we need to recognize that all the power we hold is something that God has entrusted to us (other people may also have had a role in giving it to us, but the ultimate source is God). He was the one who entrusted the earth and all its resources to men and women. Those resources include power, and leaders are called to be stewards as they use their power.

How do we show that we are stewards when it comes to power? By not using our power to achieve selfish ends, but instead using it for the benefit of all, and particularly for those who are vulnerable and disadvantaged. As human beings whom God has made responsible for the management of creation, we have a God-given responsibility to make sure that earth's resources are equitably distributed. The strongest and fastest should use their power and influence to help the weakest and slowest. When the godly lead, justice should prevail, poverty should be alleviated, and widows and orphans should be taken care of. These are the ways in which we should measure a leader's effectiveness. Leaders should not leave chaos in their wake, but rather order and beauty.

In saying that power should be used for the benefit of the poor and disadvantaged, I am not saying that they are less sinful than the rich and powerful. Both groups are sinful. But the sin of the rich and powerful often involves using the resources they have to take advantage of and oppress the poor. With fewer resources, the poor are vulnerable and urgently need to be helped, liberated and empowered.

It might not have been necessary to stress this point in a traditional African culture where there was a strong sense of community and people helped one another. But today, we are far more individualistic, and more inclined to use our power selfishly. So we need to keep reminding ourselves that God will want to know how we have used the power he gave us, whatever form it took. We must not assume that we deserve our positions, possessions and privileges because of our intelligence or our hard work or our manoeuvring at work or in politics. Those factors may have played a role – but who gave you your intelligence or blessed your work? Others may have worked equally hard without achieving material success.

Wise leaders ask God what to do with what he entrusts to them. Foolish leaders fail to appreciate that there is a God in heaven to whom all shall give an account, "for we must all appear before the judgment seat of Christ, so that each of us may receive what is due us for the things done while in the body, whether good or bad" (2 Cor 5:10).

Jesus' teaching on stewardship

Jesus told a number of parables that illustrate stewardship by telling us how God expects us to lead using the various resources at our disposal. We do not have space to discuss them all here, but you would do well to read the following parables while thinking carefully about what they teach about stewardship:

> The Birds in the Sky and Flowers in the Field – Matthew 6:25–34
> The Hidden Treasure – Matthew 13:44
> The Costly Pearl – Matthew 13:45–46
> The Feeding of the Multitude – John 6:1–15
> The Unmerciful Servant – Matthew 18:23–35
> The Rich Young Man – Matthew 19:16–24
> The Generous Employer – Matthew 20:1–16
> The Wicked Tenants – Matthew 21:33–46; Mark 12:1–12; Luke 20:9–19
> The Servant Entrusted with Supervision – Matthew 24:45–51; Luke 12:42–46
> The Talents – Matthew 25:14–30; Luke 19:12–27
> The Widow's Mite – Mark 12:41–44
> The Good Samaritan – Luke 10:25–37
> The Friend at Midnight – Luke 11:5–8
> The Rich Fool – Luke 12:16–21
> The Vigilant and Faithful Servants – Luke 12:35–48
> The Barren Fig Tree – Luke 13:6–9
> The Tower Builder – Luke 14:28–33
> The Lost Coin – Luke 15:8–10
> The Prodigal Son – Luke 15:11–32
> The Unjust Steward – Luke 16:1–9[2]

---

[2] Archdiocese of St Louis, "Teaching Stewardship through the Parables: Office of Stewardship and the Annual Catholic Appeal," accessed February 28, 2017, http://archstl.org/stewardship/page/

Of all the parables, the most difficult to understand is the parable of the Unjust Steward. The difficulty is that after describing a totally corrupt and unethical manager, Jesus commends him! But a careful reading of the passage shows that Jesus did not commend the steward's mismanagement; he commended his shrewdness and brilliant planning. This steward made the most of the brief window of opportunity he had before his dismissal became public knowledge. The lesson for us is that life on earth is temporary. Our focus should be on our heavenly dwelling and the coming of the new heaven and new earth in which life will be restored to what God originally intended it to be. (If you doubt this, compare the first two chapters of the book of Genesis and the last two chapters of the book of Revelation, and you see that the new creation is a restoration of the old creation to its original perfect state.)

The principle from the beginning was that human management of the physical realm would accomplish spiritual goals. As stewards, our goal is not to maximize our enjoyment of life on earth but to make maximum use of what God gives so that we can be a blessing to others, and so bring many to a knowledge of the God who is revealed in the things we do and say.

Stewardship in ancient Israel

God intended the ancient nation of Israel to be a model nation that would be a testimony to the rest of the world. This is what Jonah failed to see in his generation, and what we as African Christians are at risk of missing in our generation. One of the practical ways in which Israel was to be different from the rest of the world was in the way it handled material wealth. God set out his instructions for the nation in the biblical book of Deuteronomy. This book contains Moses' final words to Israel just before they entered the land of promise. He was passing on God's instructions about the kind of nation he wanted them to be. Since Old Testament Israel was meant to be an example of how a nation under submission to God lives, this book provides us with a template of the kind of society God wants to build. True, some of the details will differ because we live in a very different era, but the principles set out in Deuteronomy are still relevant today.

---

teaching-stewardship-through-parables.

When it comes to the area of wealth, its acquisition and disbursement, Deuteronomy shows us that wealth is expected to be for the benefit of all. It is God who gives the power to acquire wealth and he expects those who have great wealth not to see themselves as its owners but as his trustees and stewards. They are to manage and distribute it for his glory. He specifically reminded the Israelites, "You may say to yourself, 'My power and the strength of my hands have produced this wealth for me.' But remember the LORD your God, for it is he who gives you the ability to produce wealth" (Deut 8:17–18).

Deuteronomy 15 has some interesting things to say about the issue of poverty. In 15:4 we read, "there need be no poor people among you, for in the land the LORD your God is giving you to possess as your inheritance, he will richly bless you." Yet strangely, 15:11 seems to contradict this, for it says, "there will always be poor people in the land." Jesus quoted that verse when he said, "The poor you will always have with you" (Matt 26:11). Why this contradiction?

A closer reading of Deuteronomy will open our eyes to what it means. Look at the second half of 15:11: "Therefore I command you to be openhanded toward your fellow Israelites who are poor and needy in your land." God expects those with abundance to use their resources to help the needy. The opening verses of the chapter also talk about the Sabbath year when all debts were to be cancelled, making the rich poorer and the poor richer (Deut 15:1–2).

Robert Linthicum has this to say about that chapter,

> Deuteronomy 15 actually states three things about poverty. First, poverty is wrong and should be eliminated from God's nation (Deut 15:4). Second, the fact is that no matter how you work to eliminate poverty, "there will never cease to be some in need on the earth" (Deut 15:11). Therefore, third, "I ... command you, 'Open your hand to the poor and needy neighbor in your land'" (Deut 15:11). Everyone in the land is to work for the eradication of poverty by the way the people and systems (of power) manage their wealth. The elimination of poverty in the nation is to be the primary agenda.[3]

---

[3] Robert Linthicum, *Transforming Power: Biblical Strategies for Making a Difference in Your Community* (Downers Grove: IVP, 2005), 32.

There are several ways in which poverty can be eliminated, but all are based on the more powerful using their power and influence to serve the less powerful. When the powerful are greedy and choose to plunder, the result is what we see in Africa. Greedy people both within and outside Africa selfishly grab resources for themselves and impoverish others. It is tragic when people born into such abundance as Africa holds still live in abject poverty.

While it is easy for us to point fingers at those who hold political power, we should also recognize that we ourselves hold power, as discussed earlier. So we need to ask ourselves about our own values. How many rooms do I actually need in my house? How many cars do I need to own? How much clothing do I need, and how many pairs of shoes? What can I do to be openhanded to the poor?

Christians' use of wealth

Christian teaching on wealth tends to go to two extremes, both of which are distortions. One extreme is to say that Christians should be poor, so that the ideal Christian is someone who goes into a monastery, takes vows of poverty and totally gets out of the world. The other extreme, which is far more popular today, is to desire abundant prosperity, claiming that one has a right to do so because one is "the king's kid". The biblical position is in the middle. It understands that God has given us enough for all. We are to be good stewards of the earth's resources and manage them to help others.

We all know that in any society there are some who have the ability to create wealth. These gifted people should be encouraged to maximize their potential, but also to recognise that what they do with that wealth affects life in that society. It is sad to see a society where the few who are able to make money hoard it and do not find a way of sharing their excess wealth. They should be the ones to create employment for the less gifted. They are the fast and strong ones; they should remember their slow and weak brothers and sisters. For example, they could set up companies to provide employment for others, as Bill Gates and Steve Jobs have done. It is interesting to note that the word company comes from two Latin words, *cum* (together) and *panis* (bread). Companies were therefore originally places to have bread together. Africa needs people who will remember our communal values so that we can again eat bread together; there is enough for all.

The great preacher John Wesley was not a wealthy man when he adopted an intriguing personal financial model. He made a decision to peg his lifestyle at a certain point. Any money that came to him beyond the amount required to sustain that lifestyle would be given away so that others would benefit. It would be used to provide for orphans and widows and to finance various projects. At a certain point Wesley lived on 10 percent of his income and gave away 90 percent.

In recent times, Rick Warren's book *The Purpose Driven Life* sold so many copies that his book was second only to the Bible in book sales. Overnight he became very wealthy. But Rick decided that he was happy with his lifestyle. He did not move house or buy a new car. Though he could afford a business jet, he continued flying economy. He followed Wesley's example and at one point was living on 8 percent of his income. His rationale was that God did not want him to spend all that money on himself and his family. It was to be used to help other people.

John Stott followed a similar pattern. He lived in a tiny apartment in London and used his resources to fund Langham scholars and the writing of books – like this one! All the royalties from his many books were donated to the Literature Trust.

We have a similar example of the fast and strong helping the slow and weak in Zimbabwe. Businessman Strive Masiyiwa has used his wealth to enable more than 40,000 vulnerable children to go to school. Zimbabwean society is the better because of what he has done. If only others would follow his example!

These are just a few examples of what gifted and privileged people have done for those who are less gifted and less privileged. Like Joseph of old, they used their gifts and abilities to create wealth to serve the whole community. These people are by no means perfect; they all have personal flaws. But we should emulate their example of using their resources to better the lives of others.

Joseph could have used his supernatural knowledge of what would happen over the next fourteen years to empower himself and Pharaoh, and he would have kept his job. Instead, he ensured that there was enough food not just for Egypt but also for the surrounding nations that were going to be affected by this drought.

Well, you may say, if I were a millionaire, I could be as generous as Wesley, Warren and Masiyiwa. It may be worth pointing out that all these men developed the habit of giving and helping others long before they acquired wealth. The point is not how much you have to give. The point is to decide to adopt a certain lifestyle, to make a deliberate choice to help the slow and the weak.

The previous paragraph focused on generosity to the poor as a personal aspiration. But God's vision of there being "no poor among you" should also be the aspiration of Christian leaders. They need to recognize that discipling nations goes beyond just preaching the good news of salvation. While salvation from our sins is foundational and central, it is not the whole gospel. The gospel also needs to be preached as good news to the poor, proclaiming that the yoke of poverty will be lifted. The good news is that our God cares for the poor, the widow, the orphan and those who suffer under despotic leaders who spread mayhem and poverty. The kingdom of God advances as the effects of poor leadership are reversed through mature, godly and inspired leaders.

Christian leaders cannot preach this if they do not live it. Both they and their followers should be known for their generosity to those in need. Rather than flaunting their wealth and erecting million-dollar mansions, they should send a thousand or more children to school. They should use their abilities to set up foundations that fund things like hospitals, schools, scholarships, job-creating enterprises – anything that has potential to be sustainable and multiply should be funded from African resources that are strategically directed for that purpose.

Stewardship and Systems of Government

Up to this point, we have been talking about stewardship largely in relation to personal resources and finances. But Christian leaders need to understand that good intentions are not enough when it comes to alleviating poverty and stewarding the resources we have been given. There is a need for effective systems as we seek to maximize our efforts. Such systems can be vehicles for effective stewardship and governance.

Linthicum describes systems in this way:

A system is an organized body of people gathered together around three components: *values* that are held in common, *structures* that institutionalize those values, and *individuals* who manage and operate those institutions. All three components must exist for a system to be a system.[4]

Let us apply this definition to a specific situation: When Joseph interpreted Pharaoh's dreams, he immediately proposed a *system* that would work to mitigate the seven years of famine that he saw coming. It was important that Egypt would not starve in the time of famine and this shared *value* enabled Joseph to propose a *structure* and *individuals* within that structure who could ensure that their efforts would yield the desired results. He said,

> And now let Pharaoh look for a discerning and wise man and put him in charge of the land of Egypt. Let Pharaoh appoint commissioners over the land to take a fifth of the harvest of Egypt during the seven years of abundance. They should collect all the food of these good years that are coming and store up the grain under the authority of Pharaoh, to be kept in the cities for food. This food should be held in reserve for the country, to be used during the seven years of famine that will come upon Egypt, so that the country may not be ruined by the famine. (Gen 41:33–36)

Societies are also systems, and values, structures and individuals form the pillars on which society operates. When these three are well aligned, efforts will yield results; if any one of these three pillars is missing, a society will not stand. Grasping this point helps us to see why so many African institutions are dysfunctional.

For example, our ministerial system of governance is based on inherited colonial structures that work well in their countries of origin. They fail in Africa because of a misalignment of values and individuals. This model of governance assumes that a minister will serve the interests of the community that elected him or her into office and values stewardship of national resources for the benefit of all. However, this is not the African

---

[4] Linthicum, *Transforming Power*, 20.

understanding of what it means to be a government minister. In Africa, a government minister is not a servant to the community but its master. This is in line with the traditional African understanding that a leader is a king or a chief. Such leaders are not servants; they are served. The African cultural understanding is that a leader is a master. A leader who acts like a servant is behaving oddly and may not be a suitable candidate for leadership.

Clearly the ministerial system of government does not match the autocratic system of government that prevails in Africa. The structure of government is there, but the values and individuals are misaligned and the result is a dysfunctional system. This is the case with all colonially inherited structures; in African hands, they become dysfunctional.

Western management structures were put in place at a time when their countries were dominated by Christian values. Biblical values underpinned their societies, and the individuals in those structures functioned best when they personally upheld biblical values. Even though many of these societies have moved away from God, the values are still deeply ingrained. Without even knowing it, people behave in biblically aligned ways. Police and justice systems are strong, and so are state institutions. Those who abuse public office are quickly and efficiently dealt with. In Africa, people in influential positions are kings whom no one dares challenge for fear of the repercussions. It is better to keep quiet than face the wrath of those in authority. The absolute power of Pharaoh in Joseph's time is closer to some African leadership values than the spirit of public service.

How then are Christians who believe in servant leadership to work with autocratic leadership? Here Joseph can be our model. He did not directly challenge Pharaoh's absolute power. Instead he connected with Pharaoh at the value level and created an administrative system that would benefit Egypt even after the famine. The 20 percent tax that he introduced could, if well used as it was by Joseph, benefit the people. There is nothing wrong with taxation provided the money that comes in is used to serve the community.

Some countries like Singapore have benefited greatly from the leadership of a benevolent dictator like Lee Kuan Yew. So perhaps our goal as Christians should not be to break the culture of absolute power in African leaders, especially those who are not Christian. Instead we should seek to transform them into what are at least benevolent dictators through working to establish well-constructed systems around shared values.

There are also some traditional African leadership cultures that are more participatory and accountable and that value consensus and collaboration. For example, in the year that my family and I lived in Botswana, we learned about what the Batswana call the *kgotla*, a traditional court in which consensus-seeking strongly influences decision-making processes. The influence of this tradition has contributed to making Botswana a model of African development. Thus the University of Botswana was built through the contributions of ordinary Batswana. Everyone participated in putting it up. A sculpture of a man pulling an ox at the centre of the main campus commemorates how the common people sold their livestock to put up a university for future generations. Batswana are proud of their university, and it is handled with care because they have ownership of it.

Good traditional cultural practices can thus make African societies work. The biblical points of agreement with these cultures need to be explored to help us develop systems that work well for us.

Kleptocracy

I have suggested that we should at least work for the establishment of benevolent dictatorships. Any progress towards this goal will involve addressing a systemic vice that flourishes in Africa, namely kleptocracy, which is what bad leadership eventually degenerates into, for corrupt systems encourage illegal transactions and activities.

> Kleptocracy is when many or all the key functions of the state system – from tax collection to customs to privatization to regulation – have become so infected with corruption that legal transactions become the exception rather than the norm.[5]

Kleptocracy can also be defined as a situation "where the state is controlled and run for the benefit of an individual, or a small group,

---
[5] Thomas Friedman, *The Lexus and the Olive Tree* (New York: Anchor Books, 2000), 146.

who use their power to transfer a large fraction of society's resources to themselves".[6]

One way in which we could fight kleptocracy is by working to create a strong system of taxation. When the taxation system is weak, there is no accountability and rampant leakage of resources can take place without detection. So we should encourage officials in the tax office to start asking awkward questions of everybody, including government officials. Everyone should be expected to give an annual account of any private assets they have acquired and the source of the funding used to acquire those assets. People who amass assets and wealth must be able to show that they did it legally. If someone suddenly has wealth and assets that far exceed their income, it can justifiably be assumed that they are stealing. Among government workers this stealing often takes the form of taking state resources for their individual use.

Kleptocracy flourishes when those who see injustice do nothing to stop it but instead facilitate it. Those who see the corruption are sometimes benefiting so much from the system that they are not prepared to say anything. This attitude and practice of quietly benefiting are infectious. Why be a hero and die for it? Better to go with the flow and try and reap some benefit, if possible. Can Christians be persuaded to go against the flow?

Kleptocracy harms Africa, but it benefits the international monetary systems that control global wealth because African money generally finds its way back to them. African writer and academic, George Kinoti has observed that the international economic system contributes greatly to the impoverishment and underdevelopment of Africa and that the present world economic order unjustly serves to keep the North rich and powerful by oppressively exploiting the poor and powerless South. He comments:

> I do not object to the conditions being attached to aid that are making life difficult for many African dictators. And I know that there are people of good will in the West. But the history of the relations between African and Western nations shows that exploitation of African resources, including the people

---

[6] Daron Acemoglu, Thierry Verdier, and James A. Robinson, "Kleptocracy and Divide-and-Rule: A Model of Personal Rule", *Journal of the European Economic Association* 2, no. 2–3 (2004): 162.

themselves, is the primary motive behind much Western interest in Africa. This view is strengthened by the work of Graham Hancock who, in his recent book *Lords of Poverty*, presents evidence to show that official aid, whether bilateral or multilateral, is quite frankly a cover for the economic and political exploitation of poor nations. And what comfortable lives aid officials derive from the aid business. The future of Africa under the political and economic control of the West is bleak indeed. This situation is deeply worrying. It shames every African, whether they are Christian or not and whether they are a leader or not. It ought to be intolerable to every African.[7]

Kleptocracy benefits the thieves who steal national resources and those who control global wealth because the stolen money usually ends up in their banks.

It is very possible that if the people in Africa were to insist on transparency and the rule of law at all levels, the injustices and wickedness that seem to be a part of African politics could be abated.

Delanyo Adadevoh, a Ghanaian, once observed that Abacha and Mobutu could have jointly paid the full external debt of Ghana from the money they had amassed while in power. Ghana did not need to go to Asian and Western countries or institutions for debt cancellation. Those two African leaders could have paid for it.[8] When leaders can accumulate that much personal wealth in such impoverished countries, something has gone seriously wrong.

The brutal oppression and greed that were part of the colonial legacy in Africa have become part of African life. Those in power often do what they saw their predecessors do. Adam Hochschild compared Mobutu with King Leopold, the Belgian king who made the Congo his personal property in the late nineteenth century. Leopold regarded the colonies as nothing but places from which he could personally benefit. He mercilessly plundered the land, possibly killing as many as ten million

---

[7] George Kinoti, *Hope for Africa and What the Christian Can Do* (Nairobi: International Bible Society, 1997), 32–33.
[8] Delanyo Adadevoh, *Leading Transformation in Africa* (Orlando, FL: International Leadership Foundation, 2007).

people in the process.[9] Hochschild thinks that this man was Mobutu's leadership model.

It seems those who remove and replace oppressors do the very things that are despised in oppressors. A change of regime is not necessarily the solution. If the leaders who come into power do not hold the appropriate values, they will rule the nations they take over in the same way previous rulers did. A new leadership culture is desperately needed. George Ayittey observes:

> Most of the opposition leaders in Africa are themselves closet dictators, exhibiting the same tyrannical tendencies they so loudly denounce in the leaders they hope to replace... . It is true that some opposition leaders have endured great personal suffering: detention, torture, exile, loss of employment, property, and so forth. It may sound callous, but that gives them no ownership rights over the presidency of the country. Winning independence for an African country or saving a country from a corrupt and despotic regime gives no one the right to impose himself on a country. It is the people of the country who must decide who should rule them.[10]

Several African nations fall into the category of kleptocracies. A kleptocracy is a very unpleasant place in which to live; people want to leave the chaos and find a more orderly environment. Investors take their money out, and the poverty cycle continues. Until the scourge of kleptocracy is removed, nations will be driven into deeper and deeper poverty.

A day of reckoning is needed, and it will only come when a critical mass of people decide to take charge and stop the rot. For corruption to be weeded out, a strong statement needs to be made. This can only be done when those who have power and are stealing national resources are exposed and the nation recovers what was taken. The leadership bar must be raised higher; a new culture is needed and a new day needs to come. This scourge and disease must be driven out of our land. Its cure is transparency and accountability. Kleptocracy is a systemic evil; to

---

[9] Hochschild, *King Leopold's Ghost*, 233.
[10] George B. N. Ayittey, *Africa Betrayed* (New York: St. Martin's Press, 1992), 297–298.

reverse it our values, our structures and the people who occupy positions in those structures need to be re-examined and re-aligned.

Sycophancy

The second vice that African Christian leaders need to address is sycophancy. African culture is generally respectful and honouring of its leaders. That is good – until it is exploited by unscrupulous individuals.

Sycophancy goes with any kind of leadership because leadership is very closely related to followership. That is why a leader who functions very well in one environment with a certain group of followers may be totally inept with another group of followers.

People who have studied the leader–follower dynamic have noted the difference between effective followers and sycophantic followers. The ideal follower is the effective follower. Ira Chaleff, who is an authority in the field of followership studies, says, "I find it tragic that able leaders who fall dramatically from grace often share a common experience: their closest followers have long been aware of their fatal flaw and were unsuccessful in getting the leader to deal with it."[11] He explains one of the reasons for this phenomenon:

> The situation in which power appears to reside entirely with the leader is very dangerous both for the follower, who can be ruined at the leader's whim, and for the leader, whose followers become sycophantic … Sycophants act according to what they have learned is expected of them in a situation. They do not observe or think well for themselves, and often fail to take appropriate actions. This hurts the leader and the organization.[12]

Followers who are sycophants see what is going wrong but do not confront the leader. They so want to please the leader that even when they can see abuses of power they leave them unchecked, perhaps for fear that they themselves will become victims of abuse if the leader turns

---

[11] Ira Chaleff, *The Courageous Follower*, 2nd ed. (San Francisco: Berret-Koehler, 2003), 117.
[12] Chaleff, *The Courageous Follower*, 17–18.

on them. Or they may be gaining so much from the relationship that they feel powerless to confront the leader as they have too much to lose.

When an organization or society goes wrong, people often blame the leader, but this might not be the real problem. The problem might actually be the quality of followers. Leaders will often test boundaries, and they know what they can get away with. In some situations, and around some people, they know they will be censured, whereas in other cases they know that anything goes and they can get their way. Courageous followers are able to stand up and stop leaders when they begin to go in a wrong direction. If they cannot stop the leader from going in that direction, they have the courage to dissociate themselves from the situation by resigning and in some cases publicly exposing what needs to be exposed.

A clear understanding of the vision and values of an organization or society are key to fruitful and successful leader–follower relationships. If, for example, an organization is established to mine minerals, the wealth it produces should be used to make life better for the whole of the society. This should be one of the organizational values. When a follower sees that looting is going on, he or she should point the leadership back to the organization's values and insist on compliance. If no compliance is forthcoming, the follower should resign and blow the whistle. Or, take the example of the police, who should uphold justice and protect the citizenry from unlawful elements that might cause them harm through theft or physical injury. When the police force is used to inflict harm on innocent people or turns a blind eye when criminals rape and maim, courageous followership demands that someone in the police system stand up and say no. Sycophants will look the other way, but courageous followers will stop the rot.

In Africa, the police are sometimes co-opted by political parties. But effective followers should not tolerate party politics that encourage violence.

> The most difficult and dangerous situation occurs when the abuse of power is violent and society's legal mechanisms for correcting it have been corrupted by the abusers. Opposition must be bold and imaginative to counter the use of violent force by mobilizing the overwhelming force of public opinion

against it. Electronic media, which can focus the whole world's attention on an abuse of power, may be shifting the advantage to such opposition.[13]

Quality followership at all levels and in all societal structures is needed if the scourge of violence is to be removed from our society. The culture of violence will not end if people do not rise above their fears and courageously refuse to be part of the corrupted system.

Courageous followers are like a compass that constantly points to the direction in which we should be going. A good compass will always point true north. For Christians, and for the rest of the world though they might not know it, the true north is found in Christ. That is why the Apostle Paul told those he discipled to imitate him as he imitated Christ, or to "Follow my example as I follow the example of Christ" (1 Cor 11:1). The principle here is that Christ is the way and he is to be followed. Paul is only to be followed in so far as he follows Christ.

All human leaders are fallible, and left alone will inevitably slide into corruption. That is why no leader should have absolute power or absolute authority. Like all of us, leaders need to be held accountable to and reminded of a standard. Good followers set parameters, saying "This is how we want to be led", and then hold the leader to that standard. If the leader violates the boundaries set, he or she is censured.

That, of course, is the ideal situation. But what we see in both the church and society at large is that some leaders act with impunity and nobody seems able to control them. They throw off all restraint and go their own way. They are egotistical, a law unto themselves, and nobody seems strong enough to speak sense to them when they are going wrong.

While a good follower is loyal to a leader, a good follower is also able to confront that leader when certain lines are crossed. Issues of respect for human life, the welfare of children, the rule of law, and other basic moral values should not be violated while people silently watch. The best followers that any society can have are those who have a strong consciousness of right and wrong and who are willing to help the society uphold right standards by their own example and by speaking out when necessary. I can think of no better follower than one who has a vibrant

---

[13] Chaleff, *The Courageous Follower*, 183.

relationship with God and submits to him first and foremost, thereby growing in the moral and ethical standards God has given in his word for the benefit all. Good followership enables a good system to run as it should; bad followership results in corrupted systems.

Conclusion

The stewardship mandate is as much the church's calling as the Great Commission. Some may find that statement problematic, fearing that it undermines the priority of the Great Commission and tends towards a social gospel. As with all biblical doctrine, truth must be held in tension. We need to maintain a holistic understanding of salvation and Christian calling. A Christian's primary call is to respond to Christ's summons to come and follow him, that is, to become disciples. This is the primary call and remains the priority in Christian endeavours.

But once a person has become a disciple, he or she is called to work with God in accomplishing his purposes in creation. The unique gifts, passions and personality each person has should find expression in day-to-day work. We are Christians 24/7 and 365 days a year. Whatever work Christians do, and wherever they do it, it should be done unto the Lord and for his glory. Os Guinness reminds us,

> Grand Christian movements will rise and fall. Grand campaigns will be mounted and grand coalitions assembled. But all together such coordinated efforts will never match the influence of untold numbers of followers of Christ living out their callings faithfully across the vastness and complexity of modern society.[14]

The sad truth is that most Christians look more like Jonah than Joseph when it comes to the issue of stewardship. Our failure to understand the big picture and to have the same heart as God makes us selfish, even angry and bitter, seeking revenge against our enemies. Instead of being

---

[14] Os Guinness, *The Call: Finding and Fulfilling the Central Purpose of Your Life* (Nashville, TN: Thomas Nelson, 2003), 170.

loving, gracious and compassionate, seeking the best for all around, we may be guilty of using our God-given power for selfish interests.

If all Christians were like Joseph, good stewards of the resources and opportunities God gives, and if all lived like Christians should, the fulfilment of the Great Commission would be accelerated as more and more people would be eager to come to Christ. True Christian testimony would be found everywhere, as the waters cover the sea.

For Discussion

1. God provides for the wicked and righteous. What prevents us from providing for and showing kindness to our enemies?
2. Review the stewardship parables listed in this chapter and summarize the principle you derive from each of them.
3. Discuss people's general interpretation of Jesus words, "The poor you will always have among you" in the context of Matthew 26:11 and Deuteronomy 15:11.
4. Joseph's intervention in Egypt saved the most vulnerable in the land, the elderly, children and women; he was a good steward of power. How do you as an individual, family, church, community and nation respond to the weak and oppressed?
5. In what ways was Joseph an effective follower, and how is he a model for us?
6. How did Joseph work within the constraints of a very authoritarian system of government in which all in Egypt were expected to acquiesce to him and to Pharaoh?

8
GOVERNANCE AND CONFLICT TRANSFORMATION

In the previous chapter, we touched on issues of politics as we looked at issues relating to power and stewardship, but much of what was said there related to leadership in any church, business, or association. In this chapter, we will be reflecting on the issues relating specifically to politics. And yet, the section on conflict transformation does not apply only to political conflicts. It is also relevant to conflicts in our homes and in our churches and in our workplaces. All of which goes to show that our calling as Christians is a holistic one. We cannot chop our lives in separate rooms, where what we do in one room has no relation to what we do in another.

Christians and Politics

True Christian mission is not just taking the gospel to other nations. Rather, it involves interaction with culture, society and politics to transform them and bring them into alignment with God's kingdom values. Ultimately the battle is between two kingdoms – the kingdom of God and the kingdom of the world – both of which want to influence and control life on earth. Christians are thus neglecting their duty when they dismiss politics as a dirty game and surrender that whole realm to demonic influences.

One reason Christians make this mistake is that they limit politics to running for office. But while running for office is undoubtedly part of politics, at its heart politics is about demanding accountability from those in office and creating structures that enable good governance so that the piece of earth which the nation occupies can be "subdued" in the sense of Genesis 1:26–28. It is taking responsibility for governance in order to transform the economy of the nation and enable all to have a better quality of life.

But is this possible? For an answer, let us look at how Lee Kuan Yew, prime minister of Singapore from 1959 to 1990, was able to transform a country with no natural resources in one generation. He did it through vision, hard work, planning and improvization, or to put it more simply, good governance. His book *From Third World to First: The Singapore Story – 1965–2000* is one that all African national leaders ought to read. He explains how in 1965 Singapore was left to fend for itself when it was expelled from the much larger Federation of Malaya. The nation suddenly had to find its feet and chart a way forward. He describes the economic progress of Singapore since that time:

> Our climb from a per capita GDP of $400 in 1959 (when I took office as prime minister) to more than US$12,200 in 1990 (when I stepped down) and US$22,000 in 1999 took place at a time of immense political and economic changes in the world. In material terms we have left behind our Third World problems of poverty.[1]

According to the World Bank, in 2013 the per capita GDP of Singapore was $55,182. That is what good governance can accomplish. The effects of poor governance stand in stark contrast to this. In 2013, Zimbabwe's per capita GDP stood at $953,[2] and is not much different from the GDP in most African countries. A few are faring better, but some are faring worse.

The separation of religion and politics is not biblical thinking. Even to say "Jesus is King" is to make a political statement. Some, however, will quote John 18:36 and insist that Jesus' kingdom is not of this world, so justifying a theology that encourages non-engagement with

---

[1] Lee Kuan Yew, *From Third World to First: The Singapore Story – 1965–2000* (New York: HarperCollins, 2000), xiv–xv.
[2] "GDP per Capita (current US$) | Data | Table", accessed December 30, 2014, http://data.worldbank.org/indicator/NY.GDP.PCAP.CD.

worldly affairs, especially politics, by viewing the kingdom as strictly other-worldly and future. This strong futuristic orientation can result in an approach that pessimistically sees the nations as becoming worse and worse, more and more evil, and doomed to judgement and destruction. Those who hold this view argue that for Christians to go into politics is as pointless as arranging the chairs on a sinking *Titanic*.

While it is true that nations will be judged, that is not the full teaching about the kingdom of God. The kingdom is future, but it is also present. We are told to pray "Your kingdom come, your will be done on earth as it is in heaven" (Matt 6:10). The full coming of the kingdom and the perfect experience of God's rule on earth does lie in the future, but God's kingdom is already established in the hearts and lives of believers. His reign also extends to his corporate body, the church, in which believers together constitute the temple of the Holy Spirit. As his church allows him to rule and reign, obeying his commandments, loving all people, doing good to them and living in a manner worthy of their calling, the kingdom will be advanced outside the walls of the building into the community.

When Jesus introduced his ministry in the synagogue in Nazareth (Luke 4:18–19), he did not separate religion and politics.

> He declared that his ministry was to those suffering various forms of bondage and oppression, including economic oppression (poverty) physical oppression (diseases and disabilities), political oppression (injustice and oppressive rule) and demonic oppression (various forms of occult practices). These same evils plague Africa today.[3]

Alleviation of poverty, disease, disabilities, injustice and oppression is political work. Whether this is done by creating jobs, opening hospitals, paying doctors, organizing civil society to enable people to access rights they have been deprived of, or any other action for the good or betterment for society, it is a political action. In fact, once a certain level of benefit comes to a society because of whatever good people choose to do, politicians in that area will take note. The more good that is done,

---

[3] James B. Kantiok, "Christians and Politics", in *Africa Bible Commentary*, ed. Tokunboh Adeyemo (Nairobi, Kenya: WordAlive; Grand Rapids: Zondervan, 2006), 1001.

the more likely it is that the community will sympathize with and align to the values of the person or people who do good to them. The more they are hurt and oppressed by an individual or individuals, the more likely they are to turn away. People do not go back to a place where they get wounds and blows; they run away from there and look for a safe haven. That safe haven needs to be with believers and the church.

If we are puzzled about where to begin transformation and how to go about it, we should read widely and learn from the experience of others. In Singapore, for example, Lee Kuan Yew was successful in part because he identified the essential elements needed for nation building. He set about building an army from scratch, creating a financial sector, and building a fair (not a welfare) society, among other things. However, in doing all this, he was following a clear dream or vision. Victor Koh has summarized the vision and values of Singapore's founding fathers as follows:

- Building a harmonious, prosperous, multi-racial, multi-religious, social democratic society, based on justice, equality and meritocracy.
- Going from Third World to First World status in one generation.
- Eliminating the societal scourge of corruption.
- Developing a hard-working, highly productive society.
- Encouraging delayed gratification by encouraging savings.
- Promoting national self-reliance.
- Creating a clean, green and safe society.
- Creating a partnership of government, labour and business.
- Working towards employment for all.
- Providing housing for all.[4]

When these national ideals that formed the vision and values of the founding fathers are measured against biblical values, there is a clear alignment.

The Singaporean founding fathers did not just come up with a vision and leave it at that. They were committed to ensuring that what they envisioned came into being, and so they deliberately created the necessary structures to manage the development of their vision. It was

---
[4] Victor Koh, "The Singapore Story" (Transforming Leadership Seminar, Harare, June 19, 2012).

a clearly articulated vision with well-defined steps to accomplish it. Today we celebrate the accomplishment of that vision and the nation of Singapore is a model for the world.

Another example of nations that have managed to subdue their piece of earth and manage it productively is found in Havro and Santiso's *To Benefit from Plenty: Lessons from Chile and Norway*. Unlike Singapore, which has virtually no natural resources, these two countries are resource rich. Yet this alone does not guarantee success. As we know all too well in Africa, resources do not guarantee a wealthy country. Havro and Santiso address this point in what they call "the paradox of plenty – why more resources could imply lower growth":

> The effects of natural-resource wealth have been found to affect a country's economy in a wide range of patterns. In particular, it appears that such wealth is lowering economic growth, exacerbating the risk of conflict, civil war and non-democratic tendencies, and giving rise to heightened social divisions, weakened institutional capacity, poverty, inequality, corruption, negative savings rates and low levels of R&D... .
>
> The existence of weak and unreliable institutions, together with increased opportunity for acquiring spoils through lobbying activities or corruption, leads to diminished involvement in productive activities. At the same time, increased opportunity to depend on patronage politics coupled with the increased profitability ... of staying in office, the absence of fiscal controls, and greater problems of transparency and accountability contribute to ineffective governance and higher levels of corruption. Resource wealth might, for instance, trigger excessive external borrowing based on future resource income, serving the short-term popularity of the government, as well as its strength, while increasing long-term risks.[5]

The solution that they propose from studying Chile and Norway is that

> it appears that good, solid institutions – including both an incorruptible and reliable civil service and good market

---

[5] Goril Havro and Javier Santiso, *OECD Development Centre*, 2008, https://www.oecd.org/dev/41281577.pdf, pp. 7–8.

conditions – coupled with responsible and stable economic policy can help avoid the negative effects of possessing valuable underground resources.[6]

While "good solid institutions are needed", they are not enough on their own. As we saw in chapter 7 when we looked at what Linthicum had to say about values, structures and individuals, structures can enable good values and right people to operate effectively. But if the shared values are defective or if the wrong individuals occupy key positions, the system will not work and the whole enterprise will collapse sooner or later.

This means that we as a church need to have a multi-pronged approach when we enter the political field and tackle issues like these.

Christians and Conflict

Conflicts are inevitable wherever people are found, and they are not always bad. Disagreements can sharpen our thinking and bring out the best in groups or organizations. But when conflicts are not well managed they escalate, becoming violent and destructive. This is particularly likely to happen in environments where systems have collapsed and there is rampant kleptocracy and sycophancy – as there is in much of Africa. Thus religious and political conflicts on this continent often escalate. Institutions like the police and the army, which should maintain law and order, are sometimes not strong enough to contain conflict and terrorism, and in some cases they are used against the very people they should protect.

How should Christians respond when violent and destructive conflict breaks out? The New Testament offers a radical response: Love your enemies. This conflict transformation technique goes much further than the commonly taught models of conflict management.

Here are some words from Jesus' Sermon on the Mount to guide our thinking on this issue:

---

[6] Havro and Santiso, *OECD Development Centre*, 5.

> You have heard that it was said, "Eye for eye, and tooth for tooth." But I tell you, do not resist an evil person. If anyone slaps you on the right cheek, turn to them the other cheek also. And if anyone wants to sue you and take your shirt, hand over your coat as well. If anyone forces you to go one mile, go with them two miles. Give to the one who asks you, and do not turn away from the one who wants to borrow from you.
>
> You have heard that it was said, "Love your neighbour and hate your enemy." But I tell you, love your enemies and pray for those who persecute you, that you may be children of your Father in heaven. He causes his sun to rise on the evil and the good, and sends rain on the righteous and the unrighteous. If you love those who love you, what reward will you get? Are not even the tax collectors doing that? And if you greet only your own people, what are you doing more than others? Do not even pagans do that? Be perfect, therefore, as your heavenly Father is perfect. (Matt 5:38–48)

Jesus' words form the basis for the way we as Christians should react in conflict situations. We must work to transform the conflict into an opportunity to demonstrate the love, kindness, mercy and forgiveness of God. Our conduct should be such that the world stops and wonders why we respond so differently from other people. The story of Ben Freeth illustrates what I mean.

Ben Freeth was a white Zimbabwean farmer who was violently beaten and evicted from his farm, and whose father-in-law was beaten to death in the same incident. When the BBC interviewed him about his experience, this is what he had to say:

> While I was lying on the ground I remember saying to God "If it's my time, I am ready, but if you still got things for me down here, then I am ready."
>
> And very shortly after that, the verse that I have found most difficult that Jesus said in a Sermon on the Mount, which is "love your enemies and bless those who persecute you" came into my heart ... I reached out and I was bound very tightly and I had a badly fractured skull, I had lots of broken ribs and things like that. I reached out to the people

that were surrounding me in the darkness and I said "May the Lord Jesus bless you" and touched their feet, and I had this supernatural love to the people that were doing the terrible things to us, which resulted in my father-in-law's loss.[7]

He went on to say, "I believe the future will show us that just as black Americans are now considered Americans, just as white Americans are considered as Americans; we as white Africans will also eventually be considered to be Africans in the same way as black people, but the battle is still going on."

While he was being beaten, Ben Freeth somehow found the grace to pray for and bless those who did that to him. Going the extra mile, turning the other cheek and loving enemies takes supernatural emotional strength. This kind of act, which can only come from sincere faith, transforms a situation as the forces of evil are confronted with righteousness even as they temporarily seem to triumph.

I am well aware of the complexity of land issues in Zimbabwe, but Christians should never allow the situation to get so out of hand that people experience what Freeth and his family experienced. The question of who is right or wrong in a conflict is secondary to the conduct of the people during that conflict. Our conduct in the midst of conflict can turn the conflict around, transforming it into an opportunity to extend God's kingdom agenda.

It is not only economic issues that cause conflict. So does our faith. Over the centuries many Christians have been persecuted for their faith, and sometimes the persecution has escalated to physical violence. As African Christianity becomes more infused in the culture, the hostility, resistance and opposition to its growth move from verbal to physical. Whether this manifests as political or religious violence (as is happening when Muslims attack Christians), the most effective Christian response is to live out biblical principles like loving our enemies, praying for those that persecute us, giving to those who want to unjustly grab what is ours and going beyond the call of duty (going the extra mile). Doing so requires a strong conviction that a Christian should not retaliate and the supernatural strength endowed by the Holy Spirit.

---

[7] Freeth, Ben. Interview by BBC News, 2011. https://www.youtube.com/watch?v=fRoXXEExqtc.

Christians and Civil Authorities

But conflicts do not only occur at the individual level, and so we as Christians also need to think about how they should relate to civil authorities, both when in conflict with them and when in positions of power in the judiciary, the political sphere, or in the police and army. Are soldiers and police officers also to forgive and turn the other cheek?

There are two key passages of Scripture that help us in our thinking about the issue of Christians operating in or relating to civil authority. The first is Romans 13:1–7:

> Let everyone be subject to the governing authorities, for there is no authority except that which God has established. The authorities that exist have been established by God. Consequently, whoever rebels against the authority is rebelling against what God has instituted, and those who do so will bring judgment on themselves. For rulers hold no terror for those who do right, but for those who do wrong. Do you want to be free from fear of the one in authority? Then do what is right and you will be commended. For the one in authority is God's servant for your good. But if you do wrong, be afraid, for rulers do not bear the sword for no reason. They are God's servants, agents of wrath to bring punishment on the wrongdoer. Therefore, it is necessary to submit to the authorities, not only because of possible punishment but also as a matter of conscience.
>
> This is also why you pay taxes, for the authorities are God's servants, who give their full time to governing. Give to everyone what you owe them: If you owe taxes, pay taxes; if revenue, then revenue; if respect, then respect; if honour, then honour.

The second is 1 Peter 2:13–15:

> Submit yourselves for the Lord's sake to every human authority: whether to the emperor, as the supreme authority, or to governors, who are sent by him to punish those who do wrong and to commend those who do right. For it is God's

will that by doing good you should silence the ignorant talk of foolish people.

On the basis of these passages, we can make the following four statements:

1) Christians must be subject to or obey the government. God has delegated the responsibility of looking after the common good to the governing authorities. Those who are acting within the law have no need to fear them. But those who break the law are right to be afraid, for the judgements meted out by civil authorities are in a sense the human manifestation of the wrath of God. However, fear is not the only reason believers should obey the law. We should also do so because our conscience tells us that this is the right thing to do.

2) Government comes from God, for every authority, whether good or evil, comes from him. This truth is also taught in the Old Testament:

> No one from the east or the west
> or from the desert can exalt themselves.
> It is God who judges:
> He brings one down, he exalts another. (Ps 75:6–7)

Jesus made the same point when he told Pilate, "You would have no power over me if it were not given you from above" (John 19:10–11). In his sovereign design, God sometimes puts good authorities into power as a blessing, and he sometimes allows evil rulers as a trial or judgement. When we recognize that God's hand is at work through them, for Paul describes them as God's "servants", then we are to obey them for God's sake. We have to be prepared to live under the authority that he has permitted to be over us.

3) The main function of civil authorities and the government is to restrain evil. Humans tend to be sinful and selfish and to love power. These tendencies need to be restrained either by the inward voice of the Holy Spirit or by the external consequences of doing evil. And it is the civil authority that imposes these restraints. If there were no such authorities, there would be anarchy, vigilantism and mob justice – and

Africa has seen enough of these evils to know the chaos that they cause. So we need to remember that the authority behind the policeman is the judge; and that the judge is given authority by the government; and that the government derives its authority from the constitution; and that all of these ultimately derive their authority from God, who has established government to protect those who do good and are law-abiding against unrestrained evil and to restrain and punish evildoers. We could even say that while ministers of religion are a channel of God's love, mercy and grace, ministers of state are the channel of his anger at evil!

4) Christians should be good citizens. Peter was writing at a time when the emperor was a tyrant, who persecuted Christians. Yet Peter still told the Christians to be subject to him for the Lord's sake. Similarly, Jeremiah advised the Jews whom Nebuchadnezzar had carried off to Babylon that they should settle down and "seek the peace and prosperity of the city to which I have carried you into exile. Pray to the Lord for it, because if it prospers, you too will prosper" (Jer 29:7). (Note that God said that it was he who had taken them into captivity; Nebuchadnezzar was just a human vehicle that he used.) As good citizens, Christians should pay taxes. The state needs money if it is to be able to carry out its responsibilities. So we should show our respect for the office of those in government, even if we do not always feel respect for the people holding those offices. That is why in a democracy we vote for the people whose leadership we respect, but should accept the leadership of another if our candidate is defeated.

Given the nature of politics and the evils done by some politicians, Christians often have questions about this teaching. They ask whether Christians can take part in civil disobedience of any kind. Can a Christian join a protest march, or is that a sign of disrespect for authorities? In extreme cases, Christians may even feel that they need to work for the overthrow of a tyrannical and oppressive government. Is that ever permissible? These are valid questions, and so we need to look at them in more detail.

What does the Bible teach about civil disobedience?
The two passages quoted above are not the only ones we need to consider when we think about Christians and politics. They set out

general principles we must take very seriously, but they do not address every single situation that may arise. For example, Esther broke Persian law and risked her life by going into the king's presence without being summoned (Esth 4:10–16). She had to do this because there was an emergency. Similarly, there are times when we may have to break a law to achieve a greater good – for example, breaking the speed limit to save a life, or breaking down a neighbour's door to douse a fire.

The Bible also has examples of people who disobeyed the authorities and were blessed for doing so. The Hebrew midwives were blessed because they refused to obey Pharaoh's instruction to kill all Hebrew boys (Exod 1:15–21). God delivered three Jewish men who refused to obey the king's command to worship an idol (Dan 3:16–18; 6:6–10). The apostles refused to obey the authorities' instruction not to preach in Jesus' name (Acts 5:27–29). When there is a conflict between God's law and human laws, it is sometimes necessary to disobey the human laws that are designed to stop the advancement of God's kingdom.

We could argue that this principle can be extended to attempts to stop some gross evil that is entrenched in the laws. While no direct biblical examples can be cited to support this point, overwhelming logic shows that the action taken is good and right and in line with God's revealed will. For example, many in eighteenth-century Britain boycotted sugar because the sugar plantations relied on slave labour. While not civil disobedience as such, this boycott had the potential to disrupt the economy. More recently Martin Luther King endorsed non-violent civil disobedience when he encouraged black Americans to engage in actions that confronted racism, for example by going to "white's only" restaurants and ordering food. In America, Christians have also picketed abortion clinics and strip clubs.

But even such civil disobedience must be done in a Christian spirit. There should be no violence, and as far as possible the participants should respect the law. This may mean accepting the legal penalties for their actions.

Does the Bible offer any support for sedition or treason?

"Sedition" is conduct or speech inciting people to rebel against the authority of a government. "Treason" is acting to overthrow one's government or to harm or kill its leader. Some would argue that sedition and treason are justified in the face of tyranny, that is, when governments use all the forces at their disposal (the military, the police and the judiciary) against the people in order to remain in power.

There are no New Testament examples of sedition or treason. However, there are many examples of it in the Old Testament, especially during the period of the kings and prophets. For example, Elijah was instructed to anoint Hazael as king over Aram or Syria and Jehu as king over Israel (1 Kgs 19:15–18) while there were sitting kings of both those countries. Elijah did not carry out this instruction himself, but his disciple Elisha did so and thus sanctioned coups in both Aram and Israel (2 Kgs 8:7–15; 2 Kgs 9).

What typically happened in these biblical examples was that the sitting government was overthrown by leaders who were already in positions of authority (army commanders like Jehu or leaders of foreign powers like Nebuchadnezzar of Babylon). Yet in a situation where he knew that God had already anointed him as king, David twice refused to kill the Lord's anointed king (Saul), even though God had already spiritually rejected him. David chose to wait until God would physically remove Saul (1 Sam 24, 26).

Today, we can debate the hypothetical question of whether it would have been right for a Christian to kill Adolf Hitler. An example that is closer to home is the Zimbabwean war of liberation. The Rhodesian government said it was fighting against treasonous and seditious terrorists; the freedom fighters claimed to be fighting a war of liberation against tyrannical rule. Who was right? Who was wrong?

As the above example shows, treason and sedition are slippery terms, and we must be careful when using them. Above all, we need to be aware that resorting to sedition and treason to overthrow a government opens a door that may not easily be shut. It can lead to non-violent civil disobedience movements being influenced or taken over by individuals who encourage violent, rock-throwing, destructive and murderous demonstrations. We should never forget that even though our cause may be honourable, those who may be associated with it are sinners. It is all too easy to slide into behaviour that goes against all the tenets of Christianity.

In the modern world, many countries are democracies with constitutions that lay down how they are to be governed. In such countries, we should seek to express our disagreements with the government in ways that are constitutionally defensible. For example, most democratic constitutions allow for the formation of opposition parties that can take part in elections. Unfortunately, that right still needs to become respected in Africa. In some countries the very act of starting an opposition party or peacefully protesting is viewed as treasonous and seditious. Zimbabwean leaders like the late Ndabaningi Sithole, Morgan Tsvangirai and lately Pastor Evan Mawarire have all been charged with treason for exercising their constitutional right to protest or form opposition parties.

We need to work to create safe environments in which people can freely express their views and offer their ideas, and even offer themselves as potential leaders. We need to do this in the full awareness that this can be a dangerous path, for even the best intentions may be misunderstood.

Conclusion

If it is true that the government of a country reflects how the people in that land run their affairs, then the current state of governance in Africa is an indictment of how we run our affairs. Our continent is rife with chaos and all manner of destructive conflict. So we as Christians need to run our churches and our businesses and our lives well, adhering to the principles of stewardship discussed in chapter 8, so that we model the good governance that will result in well-run nations.

But Christians cannot practise these virtues in isolation from the larger society. The reality is that African Christians will inevitably be drawn into the complications and ugly conflicts of their societies. What we need are the skills to transform the conflict we encounter into opportunities to confront people with the gospel.

We as Christians should also learn not to take it upon ourselves to take revenge on those who have wronged us. The Bible tells us that vengeance belongs to the Lord (Rom 12:19) and he has established civil authorities to punish evildoers. Only in exceptional circumstances should Christians resort to civil disobedience, or even to sedition or treason. The spirit of the New Testament is that we should obey the

God- established authorities. Where at all possible we must live at peace with all people (Rom 12:18).

For Discussion

1. What political influence did Jonah and Joseph have in their day?
2. Discuss whether there any similarities and parallels between the stories of Joseph and Jonah and the story of Ben Freeth.
3. How do you feel about the Lord's instructions to turn the other cheek, go the extra mile and love your enemy?
4. Under what circumstances, if any, should Christians advocate for or support a revolt or war?

9

RESTORING AFRICA'S DIGNITY

The dignity of Africans has been undermined by glaring leadership failures in all spheres of society. It is time for us as Christians to work to restore that dignity.

In this book we have looked at Joseph as a leader and seen what he has to teach us about forgiveness and reconciliation, morality and integrity, stewardship, governance and conflict transformation. If the African church follows his example, Christians can engage with the African world and positively influence it in the direction of societal transformation. Sadly, many of us still follow the example of Jonah, rather than the example of Joseph.

Africa currently has the highest number of Christians in the world. But too many of us are content merely to attend church meetings. It is time for us to start living out biblical values not only in our personal lives but also in our politics, business, economics, government and media. We should be agents who lead transformation.

Before Joseph could become the leader God wanted him to be, he himself had to be transformed by God through the experiences he went through. We too should examine our lives to see how God is at work to transform us into mature representatives of God. Do we show by our lives what it is to be loving leaders of integrity who are not vindictive but forgiving; carefully stewarding the resources entrusted to us, and through good governance transforming long entrenched conflicts into opportunities for the church to practically demonstrate what Christianity can do to transform society? This should not be done naively but with the realization that the opposition we will face will come from societal structures that are backed by spiritual forces. The church should disciple the nations of Africa so that the social condition of the continent is consistent with the number of believers.

The lessons Joseph learned from his personal walk with God progressively affected all the spheres of life in which he operated – from his home, to Potiphar's house, prison and all Egyptian society, his walk with God shone through. The attacks he faced from his brothers and Mrs Potiphar were originally human conflicts but they took a demonic dimension when they moved from hatred to thoughts of murder in the case of the brothers and from lust to attempted rape by Mrs Potiphar.

Vices like hatred, division, greed and corruption can become systemic and, knowingly or unknowingly, they get passed on through generations, even assuming a demonic dimension. Every leader must deal with these vices if he or she is to be effective. We need leaders who are free from roots of bitterness and not demonically inspired to spread chaos and mayhem. We need leaders who have been broken by the Spirit of God and so can be channels of God's blessings.

Spiritually mature, emotionally balanced leaders need to come out of African church buildings into African society. The African church needs to help create and define African culture for future generations. Just as the Protestant Reformation and Christian influence shaped European culture and leadership practices, so a similar reformation and spiritual awakening that infuses biblical values into leadership culture is needed in Africa.

Where good African values have been lost, these need to be rediscovered and re-affirmed to create a wholesome society and restore African dignity. The vices of modern Africa are often due to both un-African and unbiblical values. The image of God in which we were created needs to be restored in Africa, and the African church is best placed to do that. Poverty, disease, disorder and violent conflicts need not be the African legacy.

We are not seeking for a Utopia in this fallen world. Sinful humans will always cause needless pain and spoil whatever efforts for good are attempted, but that is not to say we should give up, for the Bible admonishes us to be rich in good works (1 Tim 6:18).

Our good works can help to drive back the forces of evil that work against our continent. Our seemingly small efforts gain ground for God.

When all these efforts are put together, there will be a tidal wave of biblical transformation across the continent.

The African church holds the key to Africa's destiny. Like Joseph of old, she has experienced much pain due to injustices inflicted upon the people of Africa. Like Joseph, many in the African church have become powerful in their countries. In material terms, they are like kings and princes in our generation.

Africa's Christians are key to restoring African dignity. Africa's story can change if the African church will learn to use power well, acquiring it and giving it away by empowering others. Mature disciples who have learned to steward power can unlock resources for the weak and oppressed, allowing Africa to become all that God intended it to be.

It is time for us to arise and become stewards of power!

BIBLIOGRAPHY

Acemoglu, Daron, and James Robinson. *Why Nations Fail: The Origins of Power, Prosperity, and Poverty*. Reprint edition. New York: Crown Business, 2013.

Acemoglu, Daron, Thierry Verdier, and James A. Robinson. "Kleptocracy and Divide-and-Rule: A Model of Personal Rule". *Journal of the European Economic Association* 2 (2004): 162–192.

Adadevoh, Delanyo. *Leading Transformation in Africa*. Orlando, FL.: International Leadership Foundation, 2007.

———. *Moral Vision and Nation Building*. Orlando, FL.: International Leadership Foundation, 2010.

———. *Personal Life Transformation in Biblical Perspective*. Orlando, FL.: International Leadership Foundation, 2013. www.transformingleadership.com.

———. *The Whole Gospel to the Whole Person*. Orlando, FL.: International Leadership Foundation, 2012.

Adeyemo, Tokunboh, ed. *Africa Bible Commentary*. Nairobi: WordAlive; Grand Rapids: Zondervan, 2006.

———. *Africa's Enigma and Leadership Solutions*. Nairobi: WordAlive, 2009.

Agang, Sunday Bobai. *No More Cheeks to Turn?* Jos: Hippo; Grand Rapids, MI: Zondervan, 2017.

Aljazeera. 'Gambia Accuses Former President Jammeh of Stealing $50m'. *Aljazeera News*, 22 May 2017. http://www.aljazeera.com/news/2017/05/gambia-accuses-president-jammeh-stealing-50m-170522193325380.html.

Archdiocese of St Louis. "Teaching Stewardship through the Parables". Office of Stewardship and the Annual Catholic Appeal. Accessed February 28, 2017. http://archstl.org/stewardship/page/teaching-stewardship-through-parables.

Ataç, Mehmet-Ali. *The Mythology of Kingship in Neo-Assyrian Art.* Cambridge: Cambridge University Press, 2010.

Ayittey, George B. N. *Africa Betrayed.* New York: St. Martin's Press, 1992.

Berger, Sebastien. "Zimbabwe Hyperinflation 'Will Set World Record within Six Weeks,'" November 13, 2008. http://www.telegraph.co. uk/news/worldnews/africaandindianocean/zimbabwe/3453540/Zimbabwe-hyperinflation-will-set-world-record-within-six-weeks.html.

Deere, Jack. *Surprised by the Power of the Spirit.* Eastbourne: Kingsway, 1994.

Easton, M. G. *Illustrated Bible Dictionary.* New York: Cosimo Classics, 2006.

English Standard Version Study Bible. Wheaton, IL.: Crossway, 2008.

Freeth, Ben. Interview by BBC News, 2011. https://www.youtube.com/watch?v=fRoXXEExqtc.

Friedman, Thomas. *The Lexus and the Olive Tree.* New York: Anchor, 2000.

Gower, Ralph. *New Manners in Customs of Bible Times.* Chicago: Moody, 1988.

Guinness, Os. *The Call: Finding and Fulfilling the Central Purpose of Your Life.* Nashville, TN: Thomas Nelson, 2003.

Hancock, Graham. *The Lords of Poverty: The Power, Prestige, and Corruption of the International Aid Business.* Reprint. New York: Atlantic Monthly, 1994.

Havro, Goril and Javier Santiso. *To Benefit from Plenty: Lessons from Chile and Norway.* OECD Development Centre, 2008. http://www.oecd.org/dev/41281577.pdf.

Hochschild, Adam. *King Leopold's Ghost: A Story of Greed, Terror, and Heroism in Colonial Africa.* Reprint. Boston: Houghton Mifflin, 1999.

Jenkins, Philip. *The Next Christendom: The Coming of Global Christianity.* New edition. Oxford: Oxford University Press, 2003.

Kantiok, James B. "Christians and Politics". Page 1001 in *Africa Bible Commentary.* Edited by Tokunboh Adeyemo. Nairobi: WordAlive; Grand Rapids: Zondervan, 2006.

Kinoti, George. *Hope for Africa and What the Christian Can Do.* Nairobi: International Bible Society, 1997.

Koh, Victor. "The Singapore Story." Paper presented at the Transforming Leadership Seminar, Harare, June 19, 2012.

Linthicum, Robert. *Transforming Power: Biblical Strategies for Making a Difference in Your Community.* Downers Grove, IL: IVP, 2005.

Luckenbill, Daniel David. *Ancient Records of Assyria and Babylon.* Chicago: University of Chicago Press, 1927.

Mazrui, Ali A. *The African Condition: A Political Diagnosis.* New edition. London: Cambridge University Press, 1980.

Moyo, Dambisa, and Niall Ferguson. *Dead Aid: Why Aid Is Not Working and How There Is a Better Way for Africa.* Reprint. New York: Farrar, Straus and Giroux, 2010.

Mutonono, Dwight Simpson Munyaradzi, and Makoto L Mautsa. "Land". Page 290 in *Africa Bible Commentary.* Edited by Tokunboh Adeyemo. Nairobi: WordAlive; Grand Rapids: Zondervan, 2006.

Ndikumana, Léonce and James Boyce. *Africa's Odious Debts: How Foreign Loans and Capital Flight Bled a Continent.* London: Zed Books, 2011.

Noury, Valerie. "The Curse of Coltan", *New African.* April (2010): 34.

Oden, Thomas C. *How Africa Shaped the Christian Mind: Rediscovering the African Seedbed of Western Christianity.* Downers Grove, IL: IVP Academic, 2010.

———. *The African Memory of Mark: Reassessing Early Church Tradition.* Downers Grove, IL: IVP Academic, 2011.

Robertson, John. *Iraq: A History.* London: Oneworld Publications, 2015.

Stevens, R. Paul. *The Other Six Days.* Grand Rapids: Eerdmans, 1999.

World Bank. "GDP per Capita (current US$) | Data | Table." Accessed December 30, 2014. http://data.worldbank.org/indicator/NY.GDP.PCAP.CD.

Yew, Lee Kuan. *From Third World to First. The Singapore Story: 1965–2000.* New York: HarperCollins, 2000.

Printed in the USA
CPSIA information can be obtained
at www.ICGtesting.com
LVHW011611030923
757103LV00040B/796